MEDIA SECRETS
A MEDIA TRAINING
CRASH COURSE

*Get More Publicity, Look & Feel Your Best AND
Convert Interviews Into Web Traffic & Sales.
Strategies for TV, Print, Radio & Internet Media.*

Published by
Bestseller Big Business Press
New York, NY

ISBN-13: 978-1537537191
ISBN-10: 1537537199
First Printing
Printed in the United States of America

Cover image created by Ritesh Ghosh & Shutterstock.com
Back cover photo by Tye R Farrell
Interior photos by BigStockPhoto.com
Edited by Jo Allison & Kelly Grace Thomas
Composition by www.ipublicidades.com

Book Bonuses: www.MediaSecretsBook.com

Todtfeld, Jess.
Media Secrets: A Media Training Crash Course
Get More Publicity, Look & Feel Your Best AND Convert Interviews Into Web Traffic & Sales. Strategies for TV, Print, Radio & Internet Media / Jess Todtfeld

DEDICATION

To JoAnne,
the light in my life,
who has shared this wild ride with me.

You make the journey fun and worth it.

QUOTES

"Jess has helped us train more than 500 of our clients on how to be on TV and how to speak. Jess is absolutely, without a doubt, the best. If I needed to show someone how it's done I would go nowhere else. Look no further than Jess."

Nick Nanton, CEO
Celebrity Branding Agency, LLC & Emmy Award Winning Director, DNA Films

"Jess is simply the best. In a single session, he turned this hopelessly camera-shy print journalist into a media personality."

Christopher Elliott
Columnist, USA Today & The Washington Post

"I was completely blown away by what Jess does. I think he's a magician! From what I saw from my clients from the morning to the afternoon, he took the team from being confident guests to the level of paid spokespeople. It was amazing to me."

Drew Gerber Wasabi PR / Founder of PitchRate.com

"My aha moment . . . working with the media doesn't have to be difficult. I found the sound bite quote creation system very helpful and can use these techniques to improve the way I speak to clients."

Lane Schollenbarger, CPA, CFLA
Real American Financial Solutions, LLC

"I have hired Jess several times to work with my clients. He is the best media trainer in America. Period."

Rick Frishman
Publisher/PR Maven/Author101University

"Jess knows how to make CEOs look great. I received coaching from him and was also interviewed by Jess on a national business TV show. He is a professional who understands that the goal of interviews is to drive more business."

Daniel Milstein CEO, Gold Star Family of Companies
(Mortgages, Sports Agency, Publishing, Film Productions)

"Jess is a media pro and his experience actually producing television makes him an excellent addition to a PR team! He's the only practitioner I would ever trust to provide media training for my clients!"

Hillary Herskowitz
PR & Marketing Consultant

"Jess is a master at humanizing the media training process to help you shine instead of being another talking head. He's also a blast to work with. Use his tools and techniques to crystalize your message and sparkle. You'll be glad you did!"

Hanna Hasl-Kelchner, M.B.A., J.D.
No Nonsense Leadership Consultant, Corporate Speaker,
Best-Selling Author, Radio Host, D&B Top SMB Influencer

"Jess' training strategies helped me open doors to companies that I would have never been able to get in front of – if not for his wisdom, genius, common sense and assistance. His strategies simply work! Jess continues to inspire me to present better and better!

Thank you Jess!"

Lisa S. Roberts
Owner/Director at Back to Basics Concierge and Home Care Services LLC

"In 2015 my career took off. I began to get booked for more television appearances and I needed direction on how to bring my personality to life. Jess is a seasoned expert in media training. After a few classes and calls with Jess, I felt confident enough to tackle the TV World!"

Marlo Hampton
Style Expert, TV Personality, Host, and former Real Housewife of Atlanta

"When it comes to media training I highly recommend Jess. His years of experience at ABC, NBC and FOX has given him insight into not only what makes a good TV segment but what makes a good guest GREAT. I've seen Jess take an ordinary individual and turn them into a TV star by developing sound bites, and helping them to frame their message so that the viewers comprehend what it is they are trying to say."

Scott Lorenz
President, Book Publicist and Marketing Expert Westwind Communications

"Jess, a media expert of experts who freely shares his media secrets of success in this book. He not only helps you START to get covered in the media, but also helps you understand the importance of video to promote your business and build your brand."

Ramon Ray
Editor, Smart Hustle Magazine

"For the past 7 years we have used Jess for all of our media training for our clients. He is great at what he does and they all love him."

JW Dicks, CEO
Celebrity Branding Agency, LLC

"Jess is arguably the best media trainer in the country. He's intelligent, creative, engaging, and thorough – all my clients that have worked with him love him!"

Bruce Bobbins
Executive Vice President at DKC NYC

"Jess is a rarity these days. He is a person of integrity, superior skill, and great affability. I've learned – and continue to learn – so much from him. I recommend him without reservation as a media trainer and presentation expert."

Bruce Weinstein, Ph.D.
FORTUNE contributor
Speaker and Author, The Ethics Guy® / TheEthicsGuy.com

ACKNOWLEDGEMENTS

"Alone we can do so little, together we can do so much."
—HELEN KELLER

My successes are a team effort. I am grateful for all listed here for being links in the chain of my life. Each one of you has helped me to not only grow my business but to grow as a person.

Clients and strategic partners who I also consider friends:

Nick Nanton, JW Dicks, Lindsay Dicks, Greg Rollett and the DNA/ Celebrity Branding Agency team, Steve Harrison, Bill Harrison, Nick Summa and the Bradley Communications/National Publicity Summit team, Gallup, Land Rover, The Colorado Tourism Office, JCPR, Ed Keels, Dan Milstein, Icon Media Group, AAOSH, Own Energy, Rita Garza, Martha O'Gorman, The ASPCA, Christopher Elliot, Clay Dugas, Kushal Ramyad, Peter Lansky and the great folks at the United Nations, Mark Bower, Tom Martin, and to all of the great clients I can't mention because of NDAs.

MY NSA (National Speakers Association) colleagues who I always learn from:

In NY: Karen Jacobsen, Tami Evans, Ramon Ray, Trevor Perry, Diane Diresta, Jill Shiefelbein, Marquesa Pettway, Ben Wolff, Rochelle Rice, Ron Karr, Marlisa Brown, Jeffrey Hayzlett, Sylvie di Giusto, Sonia Satra, Jay Townsend, Eddie Turner, Sheila Pearl, Nancy Lynn, Casey Carpenter, Lindsey Hayzlett, Renee Rosenberg, Cathy Dolan Schweitzer, Margaret Marshall, Robert Gedaliah, Rande Davis Gedaliah, Maria Guida, Doris Boyer, Lois Barth, David Schwartz, Jayne Latz, Shemeka Brathwaite, Richard Marker, Dennis Gilbert, Mike Landrum, John Zenkewich, Darryl Davis, Regina Clark, Charlie Guarino, Tony Chatman, Ruth Brayer, Roger O. Grannis, Eddie Turner, Corey Kupfer, David Mohammed, Robert Stack, Theodore Henderson, John Garrett, Traciana Graves, Jean Stafford, Pauline Kehm, Dianne Devitt, and Marcia Berry.

NSA Across the World: Michael Goldberg, David Newman, Corey Pearlman, Jay Baer, Alan Stevens, Gideon Grunfeld, Laurie Brown, Phil Gerbyshak, Mitch Axelrod, Heather Lutze, Belinda Rosenblum, Anastasia Turchetta, Doug Devitre, Dr. Rick Goodman, Gerard Braud, Marco Aguilar, Stacy Tetschner, Laurie Guest, John Palumbo, Mark LeBlanc, Barbara Parus, Alexander Blass, David Avrin, Nancy Vogl, Mark Scharenbroich, Rob Waldo Waldman, Ed Rigsbee, Robert Bradford, Nikki Harris, Mary C Kelly, Susan Friedman, Geeta Nadkarni, Chris Price, Lethia Owens, Hayley Foster, Thom Singer, Michael Anderson, Dan Griffin, Dan Janal, Courtney Clark, Scott Cooksey, Jason Kotecki, Delatorro McNeal II, Dave Lieber, Michelle McCullough, Sheila Moore Anderson, Brian Walter, Gary Patterson, Patrick Allmond, Craig Price, Kate Delaney, Stephen Shapiro, and Allyson White Lewis.

Friends: Bruce Weinstein AKA "The Ethics Guy®," who has always been an amazing supporter and always cheers me on, Daniella Cracknell, Jocelyn Brandeis, Sam Elam, Gil Peretz, Patti Confessore, Brian Cohen (and The Long Island Speaker's Bureau), Terrie Wurzbacher, Charles DeBenedittis, Rodd Marcus, Mahesh Grossman, Roger Resnicoff, Orrin "Checkmate" Hudson, Paul Borgese, Michael Kingsley, David Harder, Sylvia LaFair, Herb Kaufman, Michael Schlager, Brian Kilmeade, Rob Scott, Deborah Berosset, Anna De Souza, Sondra Sneed, Dr. Chris Kammer, Lauren Sivan, Ron Messer, Melissa Krause, Paulina Gigante, Fred Cwerner, Matt Singerman, JR Allen, Mike Straka, Brendan Conway, Laurie Dhue, Wendy Witt, Jean Doody, Patrick Carlson, Ari Zoldan, Jamie King, Jen Groover, Gloria Farrell, and Stacy Schneider.

Public Relations Stars: Scott Lorenz, Bruce Bobbins and DKC, Amy Brownstein, Hillary Hershkowitz, Adam Handlesman, Heidi Krupp, Beth Grossman, Rick Frishman, Beth Feldman, Roland Alonzi, Robert Zimmerman, Peter Zorich, Paige Collins, Jennifer Willingham, Jennifer Connelly, Carol Graumann, Vanessa Wakeman, Sharon Fenster and PRSA, Michelle Tennent Nicholson, Drew Gerber, Shannon Nicholson, Gail Parenteau, Terri Slater, and the Czardom group on Facebook.

Mentors Through Seminars and Books: Anthony Robbins, Brian Tracy, Les Brown, Dr. Wayne Dyer, Deepak Chopra, and Robert Kiyosaki.

Bestseller Big Business Team: Ashley Peterson, Robyn Crane, Bronkar Lee, Steve Napolitan, Kelly Grace Thomas and business growth expert Trevor Crane who helped me get this book done and over the finish line.

My best friend since I was 19, Tye R Farrell, who always believed in my work, even when we were a couple of goofy kids starting out as communication majors at Hofstra University.

My family: Mom and Alan, Dad and Jackie, who are always there to support, believe in me and cheer me on.

Skyler and Miles, my two amazing boys who have gifts in them that will change the world.

JoAnne, my beautiful and talented wife who makes my world whole. None of this could have happened without you.

TABLE OF CONTENTS

INTRODUCTION

Navigating the waters of the media continues to change—and at record pace. Media training used to be focused on what a *reporter* asked you. Now it can be *anyone* who interviews you. The interview might be conducted with their smartphone, through a social app, and posted online for the world to see. A Google search can paint a different picture of your brand than you were hoping for. This is why the techniques in this book are more powerful than ever.

Plus, there is an issue with most media training programs. They tend to focus heavily on body language and a few techniques for owning the direction of the conversation. While all of that is still important, it doesn't address the number one question you should ask yourself before any media opportunity...

"What do I want to create as a result of this interview?"

This one question will give you insight into the path you must build to achieve the results you are after. I will help give you an action plan using techniques in this book.

The media landscape is constantly changing. What was effective as far as getting your message out there yesterday is simply not enough to yield the results you're seeking.

Whether you are giving an interview on TV, in print, radio, Twitter, with a blogger, on blog talk radio, on an investors conference call, via Skype, OoVoo, Zoom.us, Livestream, Ustream, Google Hangouts, Periscope . . . or commenting through, Facebook Live, Instagram, LinkedIn . . . or sending one person a video message, text, or otherwise through your smartphone, you need to be in control of what you say and how it is or could be received. This book gives you the tools to do so.

We are not limited by the old definition of *The Media: TV, Print, and Radio (Traditional Media.)* Here's what you need to add to *your own definition:* Mass communication that includes information delivered via text, picture, audio or video. Every day new platforms are being built and usually delivered via the Internet.

Our habits as consumers have changed and continue to evolve. There are still some who begin their day by watching/listening to a news/infotainment broadcast. Some read the newspaper on or after a commute to work. Some still watch the evening news. But, there are more and more that get news through Facebook, Snapchat, Twitter or news apps downloaded to their smartphone or computer. Some get their news, or better yet, *information* through YouTube videos, TED talks, clips of comedy shows, blogs, podcasts, and Reddit threads.

What time of day do these people get their news or information? Anytime.

Anytime it hits them to check. Notifications and alerts from our smart devices can get us to check a news story (even from our favorite social network) at any time of day, even as we are drifting off to sleep. *"Is the buzz of my phone important? Let me check to see what this is."* We can easily fall into the rabbit hole. While there is more digital content to contend with, there are for more opportunities for reaching people with our message. Better yet, there are far more targeted opportunities for reaching others with our message. How lucky we are to live in a time where you can target a specific message to: *soccer moms, who have a home based business, are concerned with nutrition, and live in Denver, Colorado.* The tools are there to do it. As always, we must tailor our messages appropriately.

While many people think it would be great to get on one of the top U.S. morning shows like *The Today Show or Good Morning America,* the truth is, less than six million people will be tuning in. Of those people, many will not be paying close attention, many will not be your right fit or prospect for your message, and many will be too busy or unmotivated to take action. Your target, wide-eyed audience might forget to take action once a new segment begins or a commercial break grabs their attention.

How do we deal with such a situation? The good news is, now, more than any other time, we have the most control over sharing our message with the masses and have more control over what we want to say.

Ordinary (non-traditional media talent) people often get more than six million views on one of their videos on YouTube or Facebook. This democratization of the media means more control over your content and messages you wish to share with the world. Some of these people may only get a few thousand views or a just a few hundred. But, if they are the *right* few thousand or few hundred, they have a much better chance of using the media to create their own desired outcome.

So, is it better to be in *The New York Times* or have 100,000 people share your story via Facebook or Twitter? The answer is that **both traditional and internet media are important, and best when used together.** *The NY Times* provides massive credibility, third-party endorsement, and proof that a major, established media outlet believes in you and/or what you have to say. This article can help you magnify that power if you use it on your website, in your marketing pieces, in newsletters, on social media, etc. Use it to drive people toward a positive conclusion. This conclusion can be them taking a next step in some way. That step could be buying your book or product, signing up for your newsletter, or simply getting information or your story out in the public to reach a greater amount of people. Whatever your aims and aspirations, having **clarity** over the next step will be important in achieving your goals.

You must always begin by asking yourself…

"What do I want to create as a result of these interviews or media attention?"

"What do I want people to *do?*"

This helps us create a path toward the right outcome—and likely income (if that's your aim). This book gets you to ask these questions and helps you build the path to get there.

MY STORY

More than **ten thousand hours** of work went into this book. As a veteran TV producer—thirteen years in the industry—I booked and produced more than 6,000 guest segments. As a media trainer, I have worked with thousands of people through trainings, workshops and speeches. As an occasional TV host, I offer interviewees the best techniques for looking, sounding and feeling their best (while connecting with the audience).  Through each of these experiences (as a producer, media trainer, and host), I have gained new insight into how I can best help those **who want to leverage the power of the media.**

After leaving television to start my media training company, and appearing as a guest in interviews, I found that I had an even better understanding of the *interviewee* experience. In 2009, while promoting a prior book, I set a Guinness World Record for the Most Interviews Given *(being interviewed the most times)* in 24 Hours on radio— **I booked and carried out 112 interviews (lasting five minutes or longer).** Needless to say, I have had plenty of opportunity to practice what I preach . . . and to see if the techniques in this book work. Now I want to share my best-kept *Media Secrets* with you.

My wish for you is that you take what you see in this *interactive* book and run with it. Action is what it is all about.

Here's How to Use This Book:

➢ **Read** the sections you need to implement most . . . and implement quickly.

➢ **Watch** the short videos associated with many of the ideas and be sure to listen to the *Media Training Quick Start* audio to get a quick dose of the biggest concepts immediately.

I'm so glad you've chosen to go on this journey! I look forward to hearing how this book contributed to your success. Decide, today, to use the media in the most effective and empowering way—and **use it to create more of what you want.**

Jess Todtfeld
President, Success in Media, Inc.

Check out the book bonuses and free resources at:

www.MediaSecretsBook.com

SECRETS FOR GETTING STARTED

"I don't have any limitations on what I think I could do or be."
—OPRAH WINFREY

This book has been designed around *your needs*. While I have never met you, I know you found this book because you have questions and you want answers. Most should be within these pages. Many will be added to the bonus content at MediaSecretsBook.com. Take some time to check out the extended content there.

While some people will read this cover to cover, let's face it, many of you just need answers, and fast.

Helpful Hint

You can easily skip to information you need prior to an interview.

It's okay to skim.

Slow down when you find what you need.

Remember, **this is an interactive multimedia book.** Some lessons have links to video or audio that further explains each concept. Some new angles on the concepts have grown since the book was published. This is how we keep a book (which is also a form of "media") from getting old.

How This Book Gets Better With Time

Do you see something you wish could be expanded? Go to www. MediaSecretsBook.com and let us know.

We will also be responding to media meltdowns by politicians and celebrities in the news (and explaining how you can learn from their mistakes.) On the flip side, we'll exemplify those who are *adept* and *poised* in handling the media spotlight.

Proud of an interview you gave or something you did as a result of this book? Share it with us and we'll feature you to our *Media Secrets* community.

Join the Community
www.MediaSecretsBook.com

Be Sure to Get Your Helpful BONUS Item

In the *MEDIA TRAINING QUICK START AUDIO*, I jumpstart your media training by teaching you the basic tools to help you feel more calm, comfortable and confident so that you approach the interview process with ease, AND get more of what you want from interviews.

Get Your Bonus Audio Here:

Go to: **www.MediaSecretsBook.com/quick**

First Things First

Before you even begin to go out and do interviews, **you need to ask yourself a few very important questions.** You should fill in the answers below. (Answering these questions is **critical** to your mission. If you don't know the destination, you'll never get there.)

What is my goal for my upcoming interview(s)?

(Do you just want to look and sound good or are you hoping the audience will *do something*. Do you want them to go to a website, buy your book or product? Do you want to make sure they understand your perspective on an event or idea?)

What do I need to have happen as a RESULT of the interview?

(Possible answers include: more sales, more credibility, and/or more web traffic. Looking more comfortable and confident is important, but should not be the end result you are driving towards.)

What would the Big Win look like?

How do you define Big Win?

This last question is one step beyond the results of the interviews. This includes both short and long-term success. Do you want to just look and sound better? Are you looking to get specific messages into your interview? Or, do you want to get more sales or drive more web traffic? All of the above? Write it down (above). (You can always revise your answer, but writing it down is the first step towards making it happen.)

You have to know where you're going if you're ever going to get there. You must **"Begin with the End in Mind"** as Stephen Covey says in *The 7 Habits of Highly Effective People.*

Know Your Destination

Having a clear sense of where you are heading is critical for this goal-setting process. If you don't do this, you are destined to mediocre interviews. Mediocre means that, while nothing overtly terrible happened, nothing great happened either.

YOU WILL ACTUALIZE YOUR GOALS BY HAVING A WELL-DESIGNED ROADMAP.

Most people think that media training is about having proper body language or not uttering *ums* and *ahs* while giving an interview. While both of those are important, it is also an opportunity to focus on the bigger picture. Use each interview as an opportunity to drive the audience to *take action.*

(Rest assured, I'll help you with those other issues—body language and verbal clutter—later in the book.)

What is the Destination?

One Size Does Not Fit All

If I gave you a set of rules and said that everyone had to play by them, I would be giving you terrible advice.

Your goals and outcomes are completely different if you are a/an:

➤ Corporate Spokesperson
➤ Author
➤ CEO
➤ Celebrity
➤ Politician
➤ PR professional
➤ Expert
➤ Paid contributor

You must decide which techniques and systems are relevant to you and your situation.

Some techniques will be *lifesavers* to you in interviews. Others will apply to other media situations you may not face.

Use the ones that work for where you are in the process. Skip the ones that are not for your situation.

Don't Over-Complicate

Many books and experts tend to make the idea of "media training" or "media consulting" *complicated*. However, my job—in this book and as an expert— is to constantly simplify the process.

Your job is the same. Decide what you want as a result of interviews and chart the course.

So, What Is an Interview?

You might say that, essentially, it's a conversation (most commonly between two people) where one person is asking questions and another answering.

Right?

Actually, it's more than that. Instead, I want you to think about interviews as one person asking questions, and the other answers, *but . . .* strategically injecting preplanned answers that have a goal in mind *and...* add value for BOTH parties.

And, guess what? You can do this **in an authentic way!** This process is not about putting one over on the media. It's about having more control.

What Do Most People Want?

Before starting a media training session or program, clients often tell me that they want to feel more:

➤ *relaxed*
➤ *comfortable*
➤ *confident*
➤ *in control*

Those are great goals. But, it is important to understand that there is a big difference between the way something *feels* and the way it *looks*. You can feel nervous and look completely relaxed. You can feel relaxed yet look nervous.

Here's some great news:

If you appear relaxed or comfortable and confident, the reality is, people perceive you that way (even if you don't feel it yet on the inside).

Not bad. Right?!

But don't worry; I'll show you how you can also *feel* better during interviews. Much of it has to do with practicing and using the systems in this book.

Looking the Part (then *feeling it*, too)

How do you *look* relaxed, comfortable, and confident?

There is a huge disconnect between the way an interview feels and the way it looks. Because of this, you might end with a completely different perception of what happened. Fortunately, there is an easy way to climb outside of your body and have a more objective view of what happened.

How do you do this? Record yourself, on video ... (and then watch it!).

This allows you to see what is happening, and keep making adjustments toward making it look better.

SEEING IS BELIEVING— THIS WILL PUSH YOU FORWARD MUCH FASTER.

*If you are truly interested in looking and sounding great during your interview, you **must** practice with a video camera.*

This is the only way for you to, quickly and objectively, course-correct, and begin to see yourself the way the rest of the world sees you.

This cannot happen by talking to yourself in the mirror, or by simply thinking about what you should do.

An athlete would never *just* sit and think about competing. They have to get out in a *real* situation for *practice* to work.

By the way, this technique is important whether we're talking about

> ➤ TV interviews
> ➤ Radio interviews
> ➤ Print interviews
> ➤ Internet media interviews

The data you learn from using a video camera is *golden*.

This gold will pay off in how much faster you'll improve.

Just like analyzing a golf swing, we must video record our practice.

Important to note: When you view the first few practice takes, you may not like them. That's fine; you should be glad that you made some mistakes when there was no pressure and when it didn't count. **Step one is practicing so you look relaxed, comfortable, and confident.**

Practice (on camera) LOOKING like you are confident and comfortable.

Many of you have heard the phrase "Fake it 'till you make it."

Forget "Fake it 'till you make it." I say:

ACT IT AND BECOME IT.

Clients often report after about a minute or two of acting this way, they begin to feel it as well.

The Good News

99% of my clients report after watching themselves after a first video rehearsal, that it **LOOKED far better than it felt.** That's an interesting phenomenon. It's also step one toward realizing you can actually do this.

The Bad News

You have to see yourself on camera. That means you'll hate the fact that your hair appears backwards, your voice sounds funny, you're feeling the "camera adds 10 pounds" effect. You might ask yourself, "How many cameras are on me?!" In this book I will give you techniques to deal with all of that trepidation. When critiquing yourself, you must learn how to become a *fair* critic of yourself.

This means:

➢ Notice what is actually working. *(Do more of that.)*
➢ Notice what isn't working. *(Do less of that.)*
➢ Let go of being over-judgmental about things that may not be big issues. (After reading the book, you should have a sense of what to look for and what matters most.)

This all probably seems like common sense, but people let a lot of negative thoughts in their heads become limiting factors.

Practice Is Easier Than Ever

Making a video recording of yourself is easier than ever. Video devices are built into our smartphones, computers have web cams, there is often a video feature found on many digital still cameras.

So, there's no excuse for not using this important tool to get some real data (on you!).

Steps to Feeling Better and More Prepared During Interviews

The following list contains different practices you can try if you would like to *feel* better during interview situations:

1. Prepare your messages in advance.
2. Understand The Answer System *(Chapter 4)*.
3. Practice so the first time you deliver answers, it is not during the actual interview. Not practicing and hoping everything will be perfect is really making the process much harder. Unless you are a seasoned, comfortable interviewee, not practicing is a risk no one should take.
4. Practicing with a video camera, using the playback, deciding what works and doesn't and then repeating the process until you get the desired result.
5. Experiencing interviews. *Anything new can be stressful. The more you experience the process, the better you will feel.* (You can practice privately and become more at ease during this process.)
6. Working with a media trainer. Shameless plug here, but of course working with an experienced and knowledgeable coach at your side helps you to get to your destination even faster. All of the top athletes and leaders in business have coaches by their side.
7. Listen to music that pumps you up on your way to the interview.
8. Watch the interviewer in action prior to your interview. The more you get a sense of their style, the more you can strategize on how best to handle yours. This is helping you to *eliminate the unknown*. The more we can eliminate from the unknown, the better you'll feel.

9. Put yourself in the interview location. In some circumstances you may be permitted to sit on the set of the TV show or sit/stand where you know the interview will take place. You can practice in your mind if people are close by. Being in the location, prior to the actual interview, will be a help and relax you more.

10. Visualize and experience a successful interview. Of course, it helps if you have clear messages and have practiced them, as well. Then, you will have something concrete to visualize.

11. If possible, chat with the interviewer prior to your interview. You can get a sense of where they plan to go in terms of the direction or tone of the interview. Make sure not to do this in a demanding or combative manner. Their job is to get the story and do right by their audience. Also make sure you realize that anything you say during this *pre-interview* or conversation is fair game for the actual interview. Nothing is "off-the-record."

12. Practice Power Poses.

POWER POSES HELP INCREASE TESTOSTERONE AND DECREASE CORTISOL.

Increasing testosterone, the hormone most associated with power, and decreasing cortisol, the hormone associated with stress, will definitely give you a confidence boost. Stand with your arms up in a winning "Y" position for two minutes. This is meant to be done alone and prior to the interview or you'd look plain silly. According to researcher and Harvard Business School Associate Professor, Amy Cuddy, this positioning is common not just to winners of sporting events and marathons.

Young children who have never seen this power pose do it naturally after getting something they want. Blind people who have never seen it have thrown their arms up in victory. This is even something that has been seen in the animal world with primates.

Adopting expansive, open nonverbal postures that are strongly associated with power and dominance can increase testosterone by about 20% and decrease cortisol by about 25%.

Lower energy poses will do the opposite. Wrapping your arms around your torso or hunching down will achieve the opposite result.

Gee, if only people knew this when green rooms (the waiting room used before a TV interview) were designed. While waiting, most people sit down nervously in a tight ball for 40 minutes or so prior to an interview. Not exactly a recipe for success.

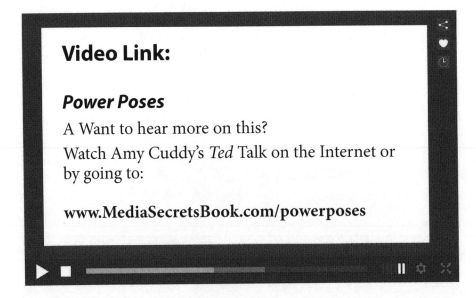

Skills + Practice
= MEDIA MASTERY

Video Link:

Power Poses

A Want to hear more on this?

Watch Amy Cuddy's *Ted* Talk on the Internet or by going to:

www.MediaSecretsBook.com/powerposes

Fear

Fear can stop us from being our best. Let's analyze how fear plays into speaking to the media—so we can get rid of it.

Is this fear a "fear of speaking?" Maybe, but that is probably simplifying what is really happening. Fear can have an immobilizing effect on us—preventing us from being our best, natural selves.

Most of the time, *Fear of the unknown* is the biggest piece of the equation. It is simply that you don't know what to expect and you don't know how it will go.

The Solution?

This book, and accompanying videos, eliminates much of the unknown. You can listen to the *Media Training Quick Start Audio* and quickly get up to speed. As for how the actual interview will go, practicing with a video camera will give you evidence that things can go your way—and is also a great way to reassure yourself that you can do this well.

Other fear factors also at play here . . .

Fear of looking bad. Practice and video evidence will help with that. Practice more than once. Our first attempt at something is rarely perfect.

Fear of forgetting. You'll learn about the "road map" in our messaging section. That will give you a system for staying on track (or message) even if you lose your place.

Fear of questions. We're back to fear of the unknown. The good news is, when you have great answers *(The Message System—Chapter 3)* and you have multiple techniques for dealing with questions *(The Answer System—Chapter 4)*, then you set yourself up for success. You no longer have to worry about questions when you have great answers ready along with a system to move there. This can also be done in an authentic way so you don't look like the politicians who get themselves into trouble for dodging questions.

Nerves. It's ok to have some nervous energy or butterflies. Use them to your advantage. Again, when applying the techniques from this book, you want to see what the result *looks like, NOT how it felt.*

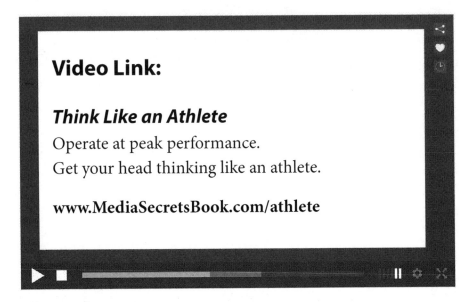

Video Link:

Think Like an Athlete
Operate at peak performance.
Get your head thinking like an athlete.

www.MediaSecretsBook.com/athlete

Feedback You May Have Received

I've worked with everyone from CEOs and high-level executives to U.N. officials and experts/ authors. And many, without fail, bring up critiques and advice they've heard along the way. Here is some of what they've shared with me:

"I once had a speech teacher that told me to sit on my hands."

"People tell me I don't move my hands enough."

"Family members have told me that they don't like my facial expressions and that I need to plan out some new ones."

My answers usually sound like this:

Family members don't always offer the best advice. What you want to do is to find some people who can look at your practice video and give helpful analysis using the guidelines in this book. Get multiple opinions, and then try some out for yourself.

While you will be learning techniques that give you more control, you still want to come off looking *real and authentic* . . . like the real you. When talking to the media, we might bring out a "bigger" version of you; but, adding anything that *looks* artificial will not usually help.

The Bottom Line On Body Language

While using your body language is a good thing, you may have too many or too little hand gestures. You may have a voice that is too high or too low. Ultimately it comes down to: *Did you get the messages you wanted into the segment/story or interview?* Are those other elements (especially, body language) adding or taking away from the interview? Usually, these are minor elements—ones you are giving more attention than they deserve. *(See chapter 7 for more in-depth focus on body language.)*

Energy Level

Having proper energy is also important. Connecting with the passion that drives you will create the best media persona.

Your *media persona* is the *on-air* version of you. Many times this can be a slightly bigger version of the *regular*/relaxed you. As you practice, this will hopefully come as close as we can get to finding the perfect intersection between your *media persona* and the *relaxed you*— equaling an authentic media personality.

When I was a TV producer, I would stay in the greenroom during the show. Part of my job was to chat with the guests and make sure they were up to speed on what would be happening. Often I would discover that they had low energy. This is not a good thing for television. (*Secret:* low-energy is not a good thing for any interview. If you don't seem passionate about your topic, no one else will be.) In those days, the only tool I had to get them into the right state of mind was to say, "Ok, before you go out there, think *Energy, Energy, Energy!*" That was hit or miss.

Now, I have a better tool. I ask clients:

"Why are you passionate about this?"

They instantly get into the state they need to be in for the interview.

PASSION = ENERGY

The 55/33/7 Rule—*or Myth?*

It's actually more of a myth than a rule, but you'll hear public speaking coaches misquoting a 1967 study.

Albert Mehrabian, a UCLA professor of psychology, actually did two studies. Essentially, the findings showed this . . . when people were asked to judge a speaker, nonverbal outweighed verbal information.

You'll often hear people quote that:

> ➢ 7% of the impact relates to the words we use
> ➢ 38% refers to voice tone and inflection
> ➢ 55% refers to the body language and/or facial expressions.

Unfortunately, in its translation over the years, the study's interpretation has become "dumbed down." When people present the findings, they don't speak about situations where this works or doesn't work.

For example, are we talking about someone giving a speech on a stage, a teacher giving a lesson, or a TV pundit pontificating? Should all be treated equally? Does a message have greater impact on you because you really need to hear it at this time in your life, or because it was delivered in a theatrical way? If a teacher says he will fail anyone who does not remember this next concept, is it his body language that is making the impact? If a TV pundit says all *insert ethnic group* should be barred from entering a country, is it her hand gestures that make the comments more memorable?

Here's What Really Matters . . . BOTH!

You must have both style and substance when you communicate. It is as simple as that.

In the *50 years* since this research was conducted, others have come to their own conclusions. Do your own analysis…

Try This Exercise:

1. Go to Ted.com and watch some of the speakers that give talks in 20 minutes or less. Or, check out a few I selected for you: www.MediaSecrets.com/ted.

2. After 7 seconds, ask yourself:
   What am I judging this person on?

3. After the speech ends, ask:
   Now what am I judging this person on?

I will give you my own analysis. *It all matters.* People make judgements on appearance and style, but the more value these speakers offer, the less important those things can become. It comes back to the **what's in it for us?** angle. If the speech (and the speaker) delivered real value to me, I'd be willing to overlook or easily get past any "snap" judgments that were made.

New Rules for Giving Energetic Interviews

If you have something interesting to say, but you tell it in a boring way . . . people won't connect with you.

If you have plenty of style with regard to voice and body language but don't have anything of value to say, people won't connect with you.

And here comes the combination:

IF YOU HAVE SOMETHING INTERESTING TO SAY, SOMETHING OF VALUE, AND YOU SAY IT WITH PASSION AND STYLE . . . PEOPLE HAVE THE BEST CHANCE FOR CONNECTING WITH YOUR MESSAGES.

Here's a postscript on this, and it is covered in-depth in *Chapter 10—Media as Marketing*. It is no longer good enough to have something interesting to say. It is no longer good enough to just have great body language or be stylish when communicating. You must also *Call People to Action*. You must tell them what they should do.

We are all familiar with the common commercial directive above. Studies show that your results dramatically increase when you ask people to do something. Sales professionals call it the **Power of the Ask.**

A Brand-New Skill

Giving a speech or presentation to a group of people is a different skill than speaking to a reporter or journalist.

When giving a speech, your goals may include keeping people awake, telling interesting stories, or to motivate or inspire.

While you might have some of those goals when talking to a journalist, your biggest goal should be *getting specific answers into the story.*

You might tell great stories or inspire the reporter, but if the final story only includes a quote that says: James Jones told us, *"Yes. I was surprised to learn of this."* (or some other boring, nonspecific quote), you will likely be disappointed with the coverage.

Leverage

Leveraging interviews means multiplying its effect.

In the "old" days, when someone would go on a show or appear in the newspaper, they had to make sure people were paying attention at that moment. If people weren't "tuning in" or reading the paper that day, it meant the exposure and promotional opportunities were lost.

Today, Internet media can give you brand-new opportunities to build on traditional media coverage.

Internet Media Vs. "Social Media."

You'll notice that I use the phrase "Internet media" in this book over the phrase "social media." The reason is . . . not all Internet media is social. Sometimes it is very one way.

If "social media" is part of your strategy, ask yourself if you are really interacting and engaging others. If not, start.

For example, let's say you had an opportunity to be a guest on the number #1 rated national TV show. Let's also suppose that seven million people are tuning in. While that number is large, look at it in comparison to the number of people in the country. It is obviously a small slice. Also, many people who you might want to see your story are at work, sleeping, or not paying full attention to the program.

Let's also think about the percentage of people that are your **pure demographic**— the target audience for your product, service, or idea. That is a smaller piece of that seven million. This is presenting some real issues in spreading your idea to the masses.

Enter . . . the Internet.

Placing traditional interviews and articles across your website(s) not only extends the shelf life of that interview, but it adds credibility. A media outlet interviewing you shows that you are a source they felt was reputable enough to show. The result is . . . trust.

Trust

Trust is a huge component when it comes to growing a business, selling something, building relationships with the public or potential clients. One might wonder if doing traditional media is still worth it. Why not just record your own interview and put it on the web. While that is not a bad idea for promotional purposes, an interview where you are featured by a known media entity brings with it an implied endorsement. When people see you, they feel they can trust you.

Secrets for Leveraging Every Media Interview Opportunity

Prior to the Interview

➤ Send your interviewer some "information and resources" to make their lives easier. This includes a *suggested* introduction. While they can introduce you however they choose, they will often use some of your wording and not forget key credits you'd love mentioned prior or during the interview itself.
➤ Send suggested questions to your interviewer.
➤ Write out how you wish to be credited (again, you are suggesting, not demanding, this).
➤ Promote your upcoming interview on Facebook, Twitter, LinkedIn, and other social media outlets where you already have professional relationships or a following.
➤ Ask "friends" on those social networks to re-post your promotion.
➤ Mention the interview in any email newsletters you many send out.
➤ Send announcements to trade organizations or those that might not just be impressed, but find value in the content.

During the Interview

➤ Give people a reason to go to your website. Give them something of value.
➤ Use the *Call to Action* strategy as discussed in the messaging section of this book. People won't ACT on what you say unless you TELL THEM TO DO SOMETHING.

After the Interview

> Collect names and email addresses in exchange for a value item on your website. This value item could be a downloadable Top 10 list, an audio, a free video, recipes, a spread sheet, etc.
> Take your interview and post a link on your website.
> Take your TV interview and put it on YouTube.
> Take your audio interview and put it on YouTube. First you must "marry" or join the audio to a graphic and turn it into a video file. (You can use Windows Movie Maker or Mac iMovie to create the new file.) The graphic should be enticing, and should have the media logo and possibly your face as well as the interviewer's face on it. If that is too difficult, sign up for a free *SoundCloud.com* account. You will be able to upload audios, marry a graphic to it, and create a finished product you can embed on a website, blog or social media page.
> Take your article and grab a still shot of it. Record an audio track where you talk about the interview. Combine the two and put it on YouTube. *(Be sure to observe copyright laws as they apply.)*
> Always make sure to properly title and "tag" your YouTube videos.
> Put any of these videos or links on a media section of your business site, your personal site (one that is *"yourname.com"*) and any other sites you have access to.
> Find any quotes from the interview that highlight you in a special way and save them for promotional use. i.e. *"Jess Todtfeld is a media training expert." —The Washington Post*
> Remember to USE these quotes in promotional materials. It gives you massive credibility in front of your potential audience.
> Use these quotes or interview snippets that you are proud of, when promoting yourself to more media outlets.

Are there more ways to multiply the effect of interviews? Absolutely.

Bonus Download:

47 Ways to Leverage Media Interviews.
www.MediaSecretsBook.com/leverage

Have interesting or unique ways that you leverage interviews? Add them to www.MediaSecretsBook.com/leverage. Check out what others are doing, too.

How to Practice

Let's simplify things. If you were learning how to play the piano or a sport, like say basketball, what would be the best way to improve your skill?

Actual practice—obvious, right?

Most people don't do the obvious. They choose to "wing it." Winging it is when someone just does what feels natural to them at the time, without a thought-out plan. Most people just sit and *think* about the interview. While that's a start, if done without actual practice, you won't become a better at anything, and that includes media interviews.

SOME PEOPLE WILL TRY TO COME UP WITH EVERY QUESTION THEY MIGHT GET ASKED.

THIS IS AN IMPOSSIBLE AND OVERLY TIME-CONSUMING TASK.

What you can do is come up with the most basic questions you might get asked, and can certainly practice those before an interview. For example, a most basic question an author is asked is, "Can you tell me about your book?" You would be shocked to hear how many authors have told me they have gotten tripped up on this type of question. It's the same as, "Tell me about yourself," in a job interview. Definitely be prepared for some form of this softball type of question. Though it is very basic, people still tend to get tripped up on it.

Steps for Practicing Interviews the Smart Way

➤ Think about what outcomes you desire. Write them down.
➤ Write out "messages" or "answers" you'd like to deliver
➤ Organize these messages into 3 categories *(You will learn this in the Messaging System, Chapter 3.)*

1	2	3

➤ Write out some "sound bites" or quotes that would work. *(You will learn more about this in the Sound Bite System, Chapter 5.)* Add them to your message grid.

> ➤ Keep in mind your Answer System techniques so that you can artfully and authentically deliver the right answers. *(You will learn more about this in the Sound Bite System, Chapter 4.)*
> ➤ PRACTICE **at least once** with a video camera.
> ➤ Playback the video and critique it. Don't forget that you want to be a fair critique of yourself.
> ➤ Decide what worked . . . do more of that.
> ➤ Decide what didn't . . . do less of that.
> ➤ In an ideal world, you would practice at least once more, if not a few times more on camera, with critique afterwards. I say *in an ideal world,* because people often say they will, but may not make the time. We are talking about five minutes of practice and five minutes of playback time here. Finding ten minutes will be invaluable to you.

If you practice this way, **you will see enormous benefits.** Additionally, you'll skip learning the hard way—*messing up* in actual interviews, and adjusting afterwards. Which do you prefer?

Training With an Expert

If you are really serious about perfecting your interview skills, have an expert on your side. Having someone to coach you through the process and get you to your destination faster is ideal.

A media trainer can help you:

➤ Learn to get specific messages into media stories
➤ Never be misquoted
➤ Drive traffic to your website
➤ Measure interview success
➤ Reduce the amount of preparation time for interviews
➤ Get the media to help you "plug" your brand, product or service
➤ Reduce tension
➤ Project leadership

Your trainer will also help you separate "the most important" elements in a critique from the trivial issues.

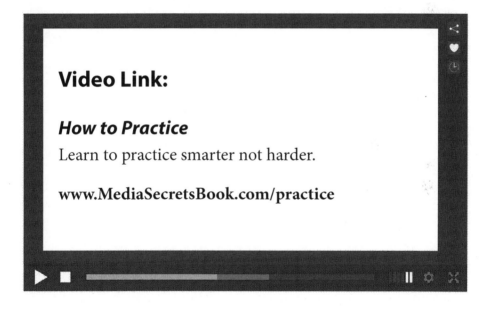

Video Link:

How to Practice

Learn to practice smarter not harder.

www.MediaSecretsBook.com/practice

SECRETS ON BREAKING THROUGH
Public Relations Secrets for Getting Booked

*"Feeling confident—or pretending that you feel confident—
is necessary to reach for opportunities."*
—SHERYL SANDBERG

35

Control With Press Releases

Simply put, if you want the media to cover you, you have to **ASK** them first.

Many people get hung up about the idea of a *press release*. They get stuck looking for the perfect format, the perfect wording, and the perfect pitch.

During my thirteen years as a TV producer, I booked and produced over 6,000 segments and, keep in mind, those 6,000 plus segments were the ones that "broke through" the clutter. Each day I would receive one to two hundred emails, stacks of mail, and at least twenty-five voicemail messages beyond what I could return. **Therefore, it is imperative that you understand how to make your press release stand out, in a stellar/ memorable way, so that it "rises above" the clutter.**

Consider these tips (on the next few pages) to ensure that your pitch/ release:

1. makes it through the *cutting through the clutter* process, and…
2. as you contemplate/figure out what would work for a particular outlet.

Know This:

It's not about having a standard template. It's about:

> ➤ Giving them what they are looking for
> ➤ Standing out
> ➤ Getting to the point
> ➤ and most importantly, getting read!

Giving them what they are looking for. What are *traditional* media people (reporters, producers, editors, etc.) looking for?

If they are TV or radio producers or bookers, they are looking for STORIES. More specifically, they are looking for GUESTS to *go along* with those STORIES.

In print, they are looking for someone to provide them with good QUOTES.

Are you a fit for that?

They are also looking for a story that:

- ➢ is interesting
- ➢ is entertaining
- ➢ is relevant
- ➢ fits that particular outlet
- ➢ adds value to their audience
- ➢ One that their boss will approve of.

That last one you have completely no control over, so just focus on the first five.

Do you have a publicist who is already helping you?

If so, use this section to create a dialogue between the two of you. Publicists have long-standing relationships with members of the media. Any way you can work together and provide support, you increase your effectiveness. Feel free to provide them a free copy of this chapter. Just send them this link: www.MediaSecretsBook.com/PRchapter

Standing Out. Here are some suggestions to help you stand out from the pack:

Let's focus on pitches sent through email since this is the easiest, most cost effective, and widely used method.

Be sure to include a subject line that contains as much pertinent information as possible.

Subject line examples:

Short Headline of Your Story – Guest Avail.

Or

Pitch: *Short Headline of Your Story*

Specific subject line example:

Pitch: Lose Weight Eating Only Fast Food (Guest Avail.)

If you do this, they will know that you are pitching a story and that there is a guest available. These are the two most important elements they're looking for. Substitute the phrase "Quotes available" in your pitch email if you are sending this to a print outlet.

In the body of your email, make sure to . . .

USE HEADLINES TO GRAB ATTENTION!
Use sub-headlines to further explain the idea.

Add just a *few sentences* explaining who you are and why you are the expert to speak about this story—a link to your bio is preferable here. If you don't have your bio on a web page, include it further down at the bottom of the email.

Add a bullet point section with information on *what you'd say in an interview.* Often I call that the *Point of View* section.

(See example on the next page.)

Include contact information at the bottom. Make sure you include a name, phone number, email address, and a cell number, if possible.

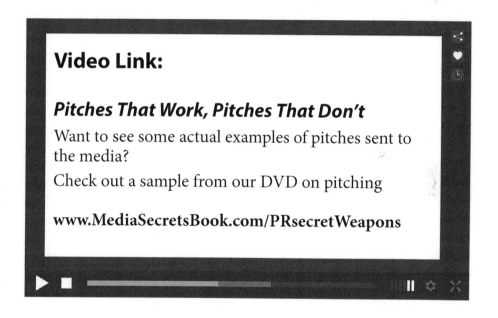

Video Link:

Pitches That Work, Pitches That Don't

Want to see some actual examples of pitches sent to the media?

Check out a sample from our DVD on pitching

www.MediaSecretsBook.com/PRsecretWeapons

Pitch email example:

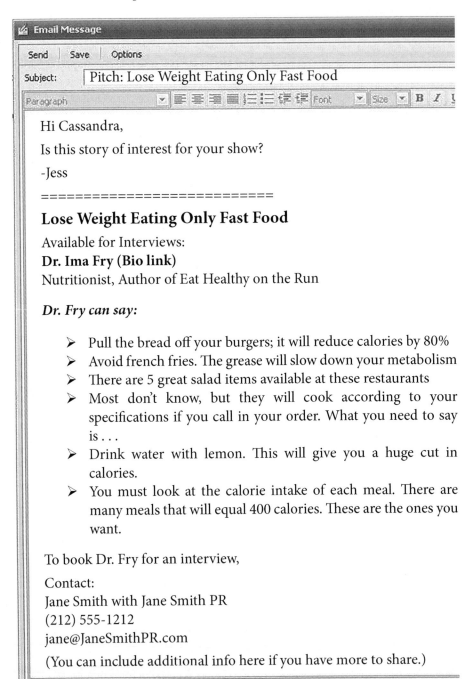

Email Message

Send | Save | Options

Subject: | Pitch: Lose Weight Eating Only Fast Food

Paragraph | ▼ | ≡ ≡ ≡ ≡ ≔ ≔ ≔ ≔ | Font | ▼ | Size | ▼ | **B** *I* |

Hi Cassandra,

Is this story of interest for your show?

-Jess

=============================

Lose Weight Eating Only Fast Food

Available for Interviews:
Dr. Ima Fry (Bio link)
Nutritionist, Author of Eat Healthy on the Run

Dr. Fry can say:

➢ Pull the bread off your burgers; it will reduce calories by 80%
➢ Avoid french fries. The grease will slow down your metabolism
➢ There are 5 great salad items available at these restaurants
➢ Most don't know, but they will cook according to your specifications if you call in your order. What you need to say is . . .
➢ Drink water with lemon. This will give you a huge cut in calories.
➢ You must look at the calorie intake of each meal. There are many meals that will equal 400 calories. These are the ones you want.

To book Dr. Fry for an interview,

Contact:
Jane Smith with Jane Smith PR
(212) 555-1212
jane@JaneSmithPR.com

(You can include additional info here if you have more to share.)

Getting to the Point. This is a big point of contention with media folks. They say that most pitches go on and on, are confusing, and, frankly, don't *get to the point.* It is important for your information to be clear, concise, and understandable. Remember this saying that sales professionals know all too well—

"A CONFUSED MIND ALWAYS SAYS NO."

So, what should you do . . . to best *get to the point?!*

➢ Use headlines
➢ Use bullet points
➢ Have someone else look over your pitch

Does it make sense? Is there anything confuting?

Tweak it, and get your most likely timely story idea out to the media.

Getting your pitch read. Okay. Let's say you do everything right. You have a very relevant, very readable pitch.

There's always the chance that your email doesn't get read!

What should you do?

Track It

There are tools to help you know who opened your email and who clicked on what. My suggestion is to use one of these tools.

Suggested Email Read Notification Tools:

➢ **Yesware.com.** Compatible with Outlook and Gmail.
➢ **MixMax.com.** Comes with some great bonus tools but only compatible with Gmail (at the time of writing this book).
➢ **ReadNotify.com.** A bit low tech and inexpensive but works— compatible with many types of email programs and clients.

I'm not a fan Microsoft Outlook®'s "read receipt" tool. Recipients sometimes get a message asking if they can agree to the notification tracking. You should use a tool that just gives you the raw data without sending the recipient notifications. This has become common place for smart marketers.

For mass/broadcast emails, such tools are available with a system like ConstantContact.com or similar.

A list of these *Read Notification* tools can be found at:
www.MediaSecretsBook.com/readreceipts

THE MESSAGE SYSTEM
Organizing Your Answers and Being Able to Deliver Them Without Being a Trained Actor

"Say what you have to say, not what you ought."
—HENRY DAVID THOREAU

What Is a Message?

A message is any communication using words or text.

What Are Media Messages?

Media messages are the specific messages you hope to get into a particular story. Anything that doesn't fit that model is "off-message."

Why a System?

The world runs on systems. Systems work together towards a bigger goal. They give structure to solving problems by making the problems another piece of the system. Systems are not just a "thing" but a set of habits or practices to help you towards a desired goal.

Creating the Perfect Media Messages for Interviews

Step 1) Get Your Important Messages on Paper.

Take a clean sheet of paper and write out all the ANSWERS you would like to deliver in your interview. (Not questions you think you'll get asked.)

Imagine if the reporter said, *"I'm too lazy to come up with great questions. Why don't you just write down the answers you like the most, and we'll use them all."* This is what I want you to be thinking during this exercise.

Now write down what you *wish* you could say in the interview. Allow yourself seven minutes for this task. If there's no time limit, it will become overwhelming. You can get a good deal of important information down in seven minutes.

Step 2) Organize Your Messages Into Three Columns.

Look for common threads so you can group them easily.

Try to give the columns headers that are short or even one word.

These three *message headings* will become your **Road Map.** It will drive you through the interview. It will keep you on track. It will give you that much-needed direction. If you are unsure of where to go next, no problem, just follow the **Road Map.**

Let me explain further. Here are three common message headings I see show up when conducting this exercise during media training workshops:

Problem	Solution	Call To Action

Look at your answers from step one (**"Get Your Important Messages on Paper"**) and see if some common categories or headings emerge. Once you've picked the headings, transfer the answers, *from step one,* into the grid.

This grid will help you deliver a three part answer . . . with depth. Often people give answers that only cover the first category. Giving answers that pull from a message in each category not only creates better answers, but ones that can stand alone.

Here are three more common media messages:

Facts	Benefits	Action *(as in Call to Action)*

Your categories can be anything you like. The goal here is to think of the 3 headings—ideally 3 words—when delivering answers.

Here are three messages that were used for a client who had a diet book:

Different (How the diet is different)	Easy	Benefits
Learning about nutrition can seem daunting We think all fast food is created equally. We are often on the go, buy fast food and feel bad about it. We wish there were better decisions but never take the time to learn.	This book makes learning about nutrition easy. Here's what you need to know . . . There are some great food choices at fast food locations. Being on the go is ok. Here's how to make smart choices. Here is an example of a great, fast food...	Decide today to learn one or two easy ways to make better food choices. Try this one special combo, it only has 400 calories Get our Top 10 list for making better food choices while on the go. It's free and on our website. Ask yourself if you... want ...

There is no right or wrong answer when picking your three category titles. Again, it's a framework for remembering what is *below* those titles.

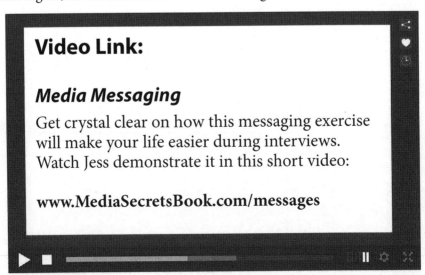

Video Link:

Media Messaging

Get crystal clear on how this messaging exercise will make your life easier during interviews. Watch Jess demonstrate it in this short video:

www.MediaSecretsBook.com/messages

Why Three?

Why three sets of answers? Wasn't it enough to have a list of great answers to deliver?

That is actually how many communications professionals help prepare CEOs and executives. They give them a briefing book with lists of answers they should say.

It has been my experience that people are **not great at memorizing pages of answers.** So, in reality, what happens is the executive uses a few of the answers and then drifts off-track for the rest of the interview. The rest of the answers are not terrible. They don't necessarily get him or her in trouble. But, not much happens in the way of motivating people who may be listening or reading . . . which is the **bigger goal.**

The Secret: You usually have enough time in interviews to deliver a three-part answer.

Having a three-part message means your answer includes: one message from column one, one message from column two, and one message from column three.

What to THINK During Interviews

Instead of focusing your energy on worrying about the questions, focus your energy on the **three words** or **headings** you came up with to create your *Road Map*.

The *Call to Action*

You may have noticed that some of the examples above contained a category called *Call to Action*. Many of the media training techniques we teach have been blended with sales techniques. *Even if you are not selling a product, you are often selling ideas.*

A *Call to Action* includes words that urge or suggest the audience—readers, viewers, listeners, etc.—to take some sort of immediate action.

Examples:
"Ask yourself this question. Do you. . . ."
"Try this one technique for yourself. . . ."
"Don't just think about making a donation. Go out and do it today."

STUDIES SHOW THAT YOU RAISE THE EFFECTIVENESS OF MAKING SOMETHING HAPPEN WHEN YOU USE A CALL TO ACTION DIRECTIVE.

This message category is also where you then include brand mentions and "plugs."

To *Plug* is to insert something, often promotional, into your interview. In the case of media interviews, it might be the name of your product, book, or company.

Most people include the plug in a completely unmotivated manner. Unmotivated "plugs" are obvious and annoying to your interviewer and the audience. Find ways to plug while "adding value" to the conversation. (*The idea* of plugging *gets a much needed revamp in Chapter 6.*)

Example:

"*Well, Paul, it is true. There are healthcare issues in this country, but what I want to talk about is that I have a book called, 10-Minute Exercises. Watch as I hold up my copy.*"

That was a plug that completely derailed the interview.

Here is a more *motivated* plug that can be used while adding value:

"Well Rebecca, it is true. Healthcare needs a solution. One piece of the equation is exercise. This was one of the motivations for writing, *10-Minute Exercises*. This is a vital piece of the solution and I'll tell you why. . . ."

Using the System

Let's say the interviewer asks this same guest why people don't eat right or exercise enough?

In her answer, she could mention part of the **PROBLEM**, then move to a **SOLUTION** and end with some sort of **CALL TO ACTION**.

1. Pick *YOUR* three categories.
2. Remember those three (category title) words or phrases.
3. Make them Your *Road Map* for success in interviews.
4. Return to this formula as much as you can in the interview.

Issues You Might Have With This System

"So you're telling us that we need to say the same thing over and over during the interview?" Won't I sound like a robot?

This is *not* what I want you to do at all.

The 1960s style of media training promoted, "Pick three messages (answers) and just say those sentences over and over." The reporter will be stuck with what you said and be forced to use it.

That doesn't fly in the 21st century. Reporters have no problem writing about how you sounded like a jerk, refused to pay attention to questions, dodged, and/or plugged inappropriately.

This is a system for organizing and remembering DIFFERENT answers that are all "on message" in terms of what you want to get into an interview.

In the *Answer System* section of this book, you'll see that you should always give a SHORT answer to the question being asked. THEN make your way to your messages (making sure that it makes sense to go there). This way, you never sound like you are *spinning* or *dodging* questions. You are just making sure **not** to spend your whole interview talking about "off-topic" messages.

For example, you may know a good deal about your local sports team. Taking up valuable interview time talking about it would be a mistake.

The same goes for talking about other areas of your business or topics you know about, but happen to be outside the three categories of answers you wrote down. Try to steer clear of points that are off-message.

More Message Techniques

Your "Opening Statement" or "Killer, First Answer." Start interviews with the perfect first answer.

Okay, let's assume you've filled out your messaging grid and you have your ROAD MAP (the three headings) in your head.

Your opening statement should include a *killer* first answer. This would be an answer that sets up what you are about and why you are there. It's your *killer* first answer because it states the most important information from your 3 categories of answers.

Step 1) You use the question as a bouncing off point.

You give a short answer that satisfies the question, and then move to your *killer first answer.*

Step 2) You take one message from each column, but they are the ones you would like to lead with. Ideally, this sets up the conversation.

It can include something about how you got to where you are. It could include the impetus for writing your book, or whatever you are there to talk about. **It is your lead-off answer.** That's it. **You've accomplished more in one answer than many do in an entire interview.**

Mixing the Message System with Your Interviewer's Questions. Use this technique to seamlessly weave in your answers.

Your interviewer might lead off with a question like:

"Why did you write this book?" or

"What do you make of this news story?" or

"Your company is doing something interesting. Can you tell us about it?

Those would be easy lead-ins.

If the interviewer asks a question that you would have expected later in the interview, you use this formula:

1. Acknowledge and mention the angle of the question.
2. Use a phrase like "It's important to note," or "Just to set things up…"
3. Say your opening statement.
4. Make your way toward the answer to the original question.

If your interviewer asks about something *off-topic*, you give a short answer that neatly ties a bow on that question and segue into your *killer first answer*. This is discussed more in the next chapter.

Stories: Where Do They Fit In?

Most media trainers do not talk about the idea of using stories in interviews. That tends to be something that works during presentations and speeches. With media interviews you usually have less time and need to get your messages across to the viewer/listener/reader and the fear is that people will use the entire time to tell one story.

You *can* use stories, **but** they must be short, 40 seconds to 1 minute. This holds true if you are talking to a print reporter over the phone. Their time is limited and they want to get the most from you in the shortest amount of time.

Stories are just "examples" that further explain your points. They can be very powerful in getting people to understand what you're saying.

Example:

SQuire Rushnell wrote a book called, *When God Winks*. After 9-11, he went on news shows talking about stories of people who had amazing things happen or just missed dying in the 9-11 tragedy due to a miracle. He had a number of these stories that were tight and ready to go. He delivered them in a compelling manner.

Is It ALWAYS Necessary to Have 3 Messages???

The simple answer is: No. I will probably anger some media trainers and consultants when saying this, but giving interviews is not a "ONE SIZE FITS ALL" equation.

Delivering an answer that has 3 parts is helpful because you have the ability and opportunity to get a message from each category into a newspaper quote or packaged news piece... all in a single answer. In a live interview, people tuning in halfway through will even hear more of the messages you want to get through.

But. . .

You might have a different set of goals for the interview.

At the end of every year, I offer up a "Media Winners & Losers" list to various outlets. My plan is simply to give them fun and interesting content and hope that I get a great intro and plug at the end.

I maximize my chances of receiving this outcome by sending a two-sentence introduction. I usually write:

Possible Introduction: (This way I'm not forcing it on them.)

Jess Todtfeld [Jess Todd-feld], President of Success In Media, a media training and communication consultant and author of Media Secrets, is here to talk about . . ." (Notice that I also made my name easier to pronounce by spelling it phonetically.)

MOST MEDIA OUTLETS WILL USE YOUR INTRO VERBATIM.

I increase my chances of receiving the plug by answering with phrases like:

"As a media consultant, if one of my clients did this I would say . . ."

"Look, as a media consultant, I work with a lot of executives and CEOs. If any of them did this, I would have to say . . . "

This is a subtle plug and signals to the interviewer that they might want to mention more about me at the end.

Does it work?

It usually works perfectly.

The Takeaway

This *Three Message System* is there to make your life easier. Trying to remember pages of answers can be daunting. Batching them like this helps make staying on-message easy and accessible.

"Winging It" Is Not a System!

Make sure you use the Message System and have a plan for answering questions in your interview. Winging it is **not** a system. The results are very shaky and you will be making your life more difficult.

Interviews Where You Are Sharing a List

Note, if you are talking about the **5 Best Ways to Save Money on Your Taxes**, the plan is very similar to the one I outlined above. Column one can contain an item on your list and could be called **"Save."** Your second column could have titles like **"How"** or **"Secret"** (as in Secret/Surprising techniques or *How* people can save money) and the third could be **Action** (as in *Call to Action.*)

Freestyle Interviews

Freestyle interviews are ones where you are invited to speak but you have no big agenda. You might be brought in as an expert. A financial analyst might be invited on a radio or TV show where the topic is money.

Your plan is different now.

The outcome you might be seeking is credibility and brand recognition. (You or your organization is the brand.) During the interview, you'll want to come off as knowledgeable and interesting.

Ideally you will be able to turn this into repeat interviews, possibly becoming a paid contributor, or just build your presence as someone the media knows and respects.

What To Worry About/ What Not To Worry About

People spend a good deal of time worrying about the questions that will be asked in an interview. This is NOT a good use of time and NOT something worth spending *too* much time worrying about.

People also spend a good deal of time thinking about what is appropriate body language. While I have included a section on this, as long as you have good energy and are *acting* natural, you are fine. Style and substance work together. You can't have one without the other.

What SHOULD You Worry About?

Things you should think about executing in an interview situation. You should:

> ➤ Make sure you know what kind of outcome(s) you would like to create.
> ➤ Chart a path towards those outcomes.
> ➤ Have a game plan.
> ➤ Use the Message System.
> ➤ Practice, even if it is just once, with a video camera.
> ➤ Actually watch the video, decide what's working…do more of that.
> ➤ Decide what isn't working . . . do less of that.

Video Link:

The Message System

Get clear on how this system can help you best include the answers you want in interviews.

www.MediaSecretsBook.com/messages

THE ANSWER SYSTEM
Secrets for Dealing With Tough Interview Questions

"Wise men speak because they have something to say;
Fools because they have to say something."
—PLATO

Bridging is not enough.

This system will help you to *move from questions* to messages you created in the last chapter. Many interviewees get stuck worrying about how to deal with the questions and are unsure how to include those best answers.

Why "Bridging" Is Not Enough

Many media trainers and "experts" talk about one technique when it comes to dealing with questions. It's called "bridging." They say, *go from the interviewer's question to where you want to go.*

Could this be any more vague?!

When I got into this field, my goal was to come up with **numerous** techniques people could easily understand and employ in their response to questions.

The goal here is **control**. How can you be in control during the interview?

Using *The Answer System*

The *Answer System* is based on the idea that we can't and shouldn't worry too much about the questions that could be asked and, instead, focus on the answers you want to be conveyed. **These numerous techniques can SPECIFICALLY get you to "where you want to go."**

What is your ultimate destination? Where are you *going* in these interviews? You are always trying to move toward answers in your 3 message categories.

What the *Answer System* Isn't

Many journalists and producers will see someone in an interview that is deliberately dodging questions. These are people choosing not to answer, and, instead, are skipping over the questions and repeating their canned messages over and over.

Want to know what media people say when they see this?
"Oh, I guess that person was media trained."

If these people *were* media trained, it certainly was not well. The idea is for people **NOT** to notice that you are using artful techniques to control the direction of the interview (this IS what I teach).

Interview techniques are a lot like TV makeup.

If you can see it, it was applied incorrectly.

The Answer System is also NOT about redundancy or beating people over the head with the same message. I call this **Burn-Bridging** because all you'll do is burn bridges with your media contacts. They will hate you for "hijacking" their interview and turning it into a one-sided "pitch fest." The *audience* will hate you for being boring or wasting their time. This is the 21st century. Those old, outdated techniques won't fly with today's savvy audiences.

Don't sound canned. You are a real human being. You want to come off the right way by sounding and *being* authentic. Giving "prepared answers" only works when they seem natural. But, if you look and sound like a robot, you will create a disconnect between you, the interviewer and the audience. Practicing with a video camera will let you know if you look or sound this way.

The Beginning of the Formula

Here it is:

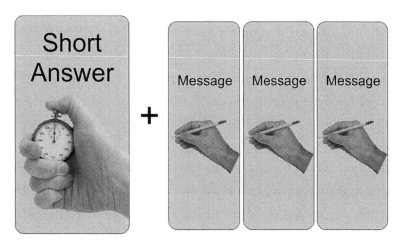

(Note: This is the basic framework. Keep reading this section to discover all the techniques that go into The Answer System.)

Example:

The reporter gives you a question. If the question is about something that doesn't directly bring you to your message . . .

YOU GIVE A SHORT ANSWER to that question

Then, deliver one short message from each of the three columns in your **Road Map.** *(See The Message System, Chapter 3.)*

If it is a question that works with your messages, you simply deliver one short message from each of the three columns in your **road map** into your response.

Your "short answer" might be as simple as "No" or "We're working on that."

Always Be Moving the Conversation

Where should you move it? Always be conscious of moving the conversation to your message points. Anything that is outside of those categories is "off-message."

The Problem with Yes and No Answers

Giving just a yes or a no answer, with nothing after it, is a missed opportunity. I rarely see this, but it is worth mentioning (except with children who often answer with just yes or no answers). Saying "Yes" or "No" only works if it is followed by ... **something interesting**—ideally . . . YOUR MESSAGES.

Not only are Yes and No responses lost opportunities on the interviewee's side, but they are also boring and make it very challenging for the interviewer to keep the conversation interesting, flowing, etc.—making you a difficult guest, and one they would hardly want to have back again.

> *Do some reporters have ulterior motives?*
>
> *Sure.*
>
> *Make sure you know what you're going into. Are they looking for facts? Are they looking to make you the villain in their story?*
>
> *You can't be misquoted if you only allow the right words to leave your lips.*

TWELVE SITUATIONAL TECHNIQUES

While this *first part* of the formula will help you with most questions, you need to be prepared for common situations. Below are 12 techniques for situations you might face (and read on, after the list, as I will explain each technique in further detail).

1. *Choose a question* when dealing with many questions being asked at once.
2. Don't repeat ANYTHING you don't want to be quoted saying.
3. Avoid enlightening the interviewer on "Everything Else You Know."
4. The Rhetorical Answer—ask a rhetorical question and answer it, too.
5. Be Clear and Easy to Understand. A confused mind always says no (even when selling ideas).
6. Use the "I don't know" technique.
7. Use the "heart" technique.
8. Reframe in your brain.
9. Keep it positive.
10. Call the moment.
11. Tie a bow on it.
12. The *"If you forget"* techniques.

TECHNIQUE #1
Choose a Question

Let's say you get asked multiple questions at once. You often see this occur with politicians. Reporters will ask about five different items at the same time.

If this happens, what do you do?
Do you juggle all the questions? Do you try to answer each in a row?

You choose the one you like the most.

When working with reporters as a producer, and later as a trainer, they have shared with me the real reason they do this. Usually they are throwing out a bunch of items and just want to see what sticks. Often, it is not some sort of devious plot or form of trickery. It's just someone hoping you'll say something interesting.

If they give you a hard time—and they don't usually do that—just say, "I'm happy to answer all of your questions, just give them to me one at a time."

In a press conference situation, you can say something to the effect of, "I think you have about five questions in there. I want to give other reporters a chance to ask questions as well, so what I *can* tell you is . . ." (Then choose the one or two you wish to answer.)

TECHNIQUE #2
Don't Repeat ANYTHING You Don't Want to Be Quoted Saying

Reporter: "Isn't it true that people who do what you do are out to take people's money?"

Interviewee: "There are a lot of people who just want to take your money, but our company has been around 100 years and our clients know we operate with integrity."

It is entirely possible that the quote that makes it into a story is: **"There are a lot of people who just want to take your money."**

Is it a misquote? No. If you said it, they can use it. This person validated the reporters concern.

In the example above, the interviewee repeated a negative phrase. Never do this. Does the famous quote, "I am not a crook," ring a bell?

What should you say?

Using your formula, the short answer could be, "I can only speak for our company" or "No." or "Ha ha." You then follow it with. . . . ***Your Messages.***

You might still follow with, "Our company has been around for 100 years, and our clients know we operate with integrity—we have the customer loyalty to prove it."

DON'T REPEAT ANYTHING YOU ARE NOT COMFORTABLE BEING QUOTED SAYING. DON'T ALLOW THEM TO PUT WORDS IN YOUR MOUTH.

TECHNIQUE #3
Avoid Enlightening the Interviewer on "Everything Else You Know"

There are two places you could go with answers. You could take the conversation toward your 3 message categories. Or . . . you could go off message and start sharing your thoughts on other subjects. This is **the land** *of everything else you know*. It is very tempting to go there. As humans, we like to show that we are knowledgeable in many areas. In interviews this is a mistake.

For example, you are doing an interview talking about a new service your company is offering. The interviewer starts asking questions about the city you're in, other companies, maybe even the Super Bowl or a current event that just happened.

What do you do?

Think about the question. Do you really need to go in-depth on this answer? Is there a way to give a short answer, and get back onto message? If the topic they want to discuss is "off-message," you want to spend the least amount of time talking about it.

Example:

Interviewer: "I know you are here to talk about your company's new product but first what did you make of the big game last night?"

Wrong Answer:

"This was a team that had a tough year. It started with injuries early on and then a bunch of losses. I was surprised that their defense decided to ..."

Correct Answer:

"Great Game, but I knew the big excitement was getting up early to be on TV with you!"

This is where the interviewer chuckles and switches gears and talks about your topic. You don't want to monopolize your time with *off-message* answers.

TECHNIQUE #4
The Rhetorical Answer

Ask your own questions . . . and answer them too!

Q: *Is it true that the tax code is confusing and people need new strategies?*

A: *"Look, should everyone know about this tax-saving strategy? Yes, they should. Are they losing money by not knowing? Absolutely."*

Your answer is a rhetorical question and, ideally, you include an answer to your own questions.

This is one of my favorite techniques. It gives you an unbelievable amount of control in interviews, and it happens to be a sound bite element as well. *(See the next chapter.)*

Special note: **You can only do this once or twice in an interview.** If you use it too much, you could be accused of "hijacking" the interview. When I was a producer, we would use that phrase when a guest was obvious about pushing their agenda on us, no matter what was asked. Notice, in the previous example, that the answer still works with the question.

TECHNIQUE #5
Be Clear and Easy to Understand

A confused mind always says, "No." This is a phrase that sales professionals often say, and it's true. Think about someone who tried to sell you something. If they weren't crystal clear, a decision to buy was not likely made by you.

The same works when selling ideas. The more you can focus in on what you are saying, and say it in a clear, easy to digest manner, the more chance you have of connecting with your audience.

Example *of what* not *to do:*

Q: *Can you tell me about your book?*

A: *"I'd like to start with the history of quantum physics, which inspired me to detail the QBMI, and then explain how that brought me to write this book about how one creates and sustains happiness."*

The problem here is there is too much information. It will probably consume the entire interview. This person is likely going off-message and going too in-depth. AND, the abbreviation might confuse people. . If you simplify your message, you will keep people's attention, reach more of the audience, and not confuse anyone. Of course, we want to do this while maintaining the integrity of your topic.

Here's a better way to answer (without being too complex):

Q: *"Can you tell me about your book?"*

A: *"Well, it's a book that can show you how to be happier. I went pretty deep, and in a number of directions, to understand what makes us tick. But, more importantly, this book details what we can do to be happier—it has to do with 9 key principles. I will be outlining a few of them today."*

We now have a crystal clear answer to the question. The interviewer and interviewee got what they wanted. The audience heard about some of the benefits, and got as a sense of what else would be coming. The interviewee steered clear of the complex and delivered a perfect answer.

TECHNIQUE #6
"I Don't Know" Technique

What if you get a question that you simply *do not know* the answer to?

You might get a question focused on specific data that you just do not have. What do you do in these situations???

It is ok to say, "I don't know," as long as you follow it with... **something you actually do know.**

For example, let's say I was asked a legal question:

Q: *"Jack, doesn't the jury have an obligation to take their time coming up with this verdict?"*

A: *"Well, I'm not an attorney, but having served on a jury I can tell you that it usually takes as long as is necessary. As a communication consultant, I recognized that the prosecutor mentioned many times that this would be a quick and easy decision. That tells me . . ."*

Notice how the beginning of the answer becomes a *jumping off point.*

Here's another example:

Q: *"Is this a bad move, politically, for this politician to say that?"*

A: *"I don't know about the politics, but I can tell you that the public knows when someone comes off less than genuine. If I was his consultant, I would advise . . ."*

TECHNIQUE #7
The "Heart" Technique

When I work with clients prepping or dealing with a crisis, they often focus a good deal on the facts, and forget to include the heart. The heart is the emotional side. How were people affected by what happened? What does this mean for the community? What does this mean for the employees of this company?

Example:

Q: *"This oil pipeline explosion has caused complete havoc, to say the least. Explain where things are currently at."*

A: *"The explosion appears to have been due to pressure build up and some faulty equipment. We have launched a full investigation to get to the bottom of this situation. It is important to mention that seven people were hurt and hospitalized. They are not just employees, but are extended members of the Faulty Oil company family. Though the accident's cause is important to us, these people are our top concern right now."*

TECHNIQUE #8
Reframe in Your Brain

Take a tough question and ask yourself, **What** are they really asking? Reframe and answer.

Q: *"Isn't it true that people in your profession are out to take people's money and just aren't reputable?"*

REFRAMING THE QUESTION (in your brain):

"How can we trust you?" or *"How can we find a trustworthy person in your profession?"*

The answer now comes from a place of helping the interviewer, educating them, and adding value. This is a far better way of handling the question (rather than being on the defensive):

A: *No. We pride ourselves on our work and how many referrals we obtain from people in the community who are highly satisfied with our service.*

In fact, tough questions like this are often just objections and concerns being voiced. If you are confident and stand by your topic, you should **welcome objections**. You should learn to love them because the better you get at dealing with these tougher questions, and turning them into positives, the more the audience will be convinced of what you are saying.

Sales professionals know this very well. Don't forget, even if you are not selling a product, you are selling ideas.

TECHNIQUE #9
Keep It Positive

Unless your branding is to be negative in some way—meaning that you're a critic or you seek out spirited debate—then keeping it positive is the way to go.

Say you get a question that is tough. It might even be an attack. As I stated earlier, you must see this as fielding objections. Objections are good. The more you can deal with them, the more people are sold on your ideas.

So you get this tough question. You have two choices—do you put on a smile, give a good answer and stand your ground? Or, do you get defensive and battle it out.

Unless you have decided that you are fine battling the interviewer, that you are fine if they quote your attacks, that you are fine coming off as angry, you should go the positive route.

Q: *"People with ideas like this are often charlatans, aren't they?!"*

A: *"It would be easy to paint everyone that way. Let's look at the facts here. What we found was . . . "*

Keeping it positive will always keep a smile on your face *(which means you are likable)* and you're not getting all caught up in the moment—like some people do—trying to fight everybody on every point. You can walk away as the person who just looks like a winner (and sounds like a winner).

Keep it positive.

TECHNIQUE #10
Call the Moment

Here's how it works. Say you were on a television show and they had a bottle of water sitting in front of you. You go to answer a question and you wave your hand and knock the bottle over.

Water is now spilling all over the desk and down the side and you are rightfully embarrassed. And you've no idea what to do. Everyone saw you do this—all eyes are on you. You need to gracefully get yourself out of it and get back on track. So, instead of ignoring it, you need to *call the moment.* You need to stop, look, smile and say, "Ah, I guess I'm really fired up about this. Sorry about that! Where were we? Alright!" and you're smiling and you're going back to your discussion.

It was a human moment. You are a human being. Those things happen. You go with it, but you call the moment.

A few years ago, I was watching a PBS broadcast of a Deepak Chopra seminar and a fly was flying around near his head. I'm sure the whole audience noticed it. Deepak, whom I have great respect for, stayed focused on his content. And, of course, the fly kept making its way back hear him.

If he had called the moment, he could have stopped and said, "Where are we, in a barn?! What's going on?!" and smiled/chuckled and it would have been the end of it. Instead, he ignored it. It was a distraction that kept returning. He even tried waving it away at one point. He could have joked that it was someone reincarnated enjoying his talk.

The lesson here . . .

Just call the moment! It'll get you out of the situation and it will keep the audience focused on why you're there and what you have to say—and not the silly fly!

TECHNIQUE #11
Tie a Bow on It

If you're talking and talking and you're trying to deliver an answer and it doesn't seem to have an end—you just keep going and don't know how to end it, what do you do?

Tie a bow on it. Sometimes, just bringing the inflection of your voice down can signal the end of a thought. You can add phrases that signal the thought has ended like ". . . and that is the basic idea."

I have had many clients who have found themselves giving an answer—talking and talking—and realize, in the playback, *"Wow, I probably should've just ended it after those first few sentences. I made my point, and then why did I keep going?"* In doing so, they muddled their point. They realized that they should have just found a place to stop talking, and tie a bow on it.

TECHNIQUE #12
The *"If You Forget"* Techniques

Let's say you are talking—giving your messages—and you forget where you were going with your point. And you think, Oh no! What am I going to do, now?! *You'd say that in your brain.* But, in actuality, here's what you do: Let's say you were giving a list of three items—and you could be numbering them or not numbering them. But for the sake of the example, you say, "Number 1 is … people should do *this*. Number 2 people should do *this other thing*. And Number 3. . . . " and you start to realize that you forgot Number 3.""Number 3 is . . ."

Instead of freezing, you could say "See numbers 1 and 2." You can say something like that and get yourself out of the trouble of what to do when you've numbered something. And if you say, "This is important. . . . That's important. . . . , and the last part is . . . See the first two!" So you can do that to get yourself out of that situation. This works.

Would this have worked for Rick Perry, U.S. Presidential candidate in 2012? During one of the presidential debates, he remarked about three agencies of government he wanted to eliminate. He was able to name the first two but could not remember the third. His answer, when asked if he really couldn't remember the third, was "No, I cannot. Oops." **Oops is not acceptable.**

While the stakes are much higher when you are running for president, it would have been better than the *Oops* answer he gave. The problem, in his situation, was his three agency answer was already known by the audience. He had already shared it in interviews and on talk shows. When running for a high office like this, there is less room for mistakes. The good news is, if you are **not** running for president, most interviewers will try to "save the interview" and help if there is a slow or awkward moment. Unless you are there to be in the hot seat, they want you to share interesting information with their audience.

Another technique in this situation:

So, say you are talking and you lose your train of thought, and you need help getting out of this jam. While you're talking and talking STOP, for a half second, and throw in this phrase: "Look, let me just bottom line it for you. . . ." or "Let me point you toward what is most important. What you need to know is . . ." Then, say something from those three message categories.

If you do that, it will get you out of those sticky situations because the interviewer and the audience all are thinking, "Oh great, he was making his way toward a point, and then stopped, like we may do in natural, normal conversation, . . . and realized that he wanted to bottom-line it for us." Now it's like you're doing a big service for the people who are listening or watching. It's a great technique and it will get you out of those situations where you forgot what you were going to say.

Here are some final thoughts on answering questions.

The toughest question that many authors say they get asked—and it's often the very first question. . . .

"Tell me about your book."

It's not even a question! It's just a statement! That's like saying, "Why don't you start talking?!" And this often stops guests in their tracks. They have no idea where to start. They are probably thinking, "Maybe I'll start at birth, and work my way to the present!" Okay, obviously that would be too much. So, if you get an open-ended question, view this, from now on, as a sign that this is an uninformed or perhaps lazy interviewer, and you now have complete control to drive the interview (and point it to where you want it to go).

I had a client who once went on a program and the interviewer said, "I'm excited to have you here! This is an important topic." And then proceeded by picking up the author's book, which actually made a creaking noise [creakkkkk!], signifying to my client that it hadn't been read at all. He instantly knew that this interviewer had no idea what was in the book, making him feel nervous. Don't be. **You can't wish for a better situation than this.** You are now in complete control during that interview.

Although I used an author example, I find that this is helpful for anyone who goes into a situation where the interviewer is either asking vague questions or not informed about what you're coming on to speak about.

What If???

The following section handles many of the "what if's" and **frequently asked questions.**

What if the interviewer attacks me? If this is a surprise to you, fall back on techniques mentioned in this chapter. Before an interview, research your interviewer and others who might be involved. If you know it will be a combative interview, it helps to practice and prepare for it. Remember, these are just objections. You want to learn to love objections, deal with them, and get people to see your point of view.

What if they ask me about politics or something else personal I would rather not disclose? Give a short answer saying that this is personal or that you don't discuss politics. Next, transition to the *long answer* portion, and move to relevant items from the Message System.

What if they ask me about something off-topic that I like talking about? Make sure to give a brief answer and try to get the interview back on track. I had an author client who was asked a question about her daughter. The interviewer knew that her daughter went to college close by. This author talked about her daughter for the next few minutes and lost some valuable air time. This book was about living the American dream. A better option would have been to deliver a short answer saying "Even my daughter is living the American dream" and then transition back to how that fits in with the book and main interview discussion.

What if they know nothing about me or my topic and leave me to my own devices? Great! Take control. Deliver information that is valuable to the audience. This does happen from time to time. The interviewer is faced with many stories in a short amount of time and only properly prepares for some of them. Again, this is a gift. Treat it that way.

What if I only get a minute or two? (Or am on with others and only get this short amount of time?) Deliver three part answers using your Message System. Deliver that killer first answer, give value and leave 'em wanting more. Hopefully your website will be "plugged."

What if I go out there, I don't mess it up, but I don't really do anything to stand out? This is one of the biggest problems I see. What happens next is … nothing. You did not create any positive brand mentions. You didn't add value for the audience. You didn't create excitement that led people to find out more about you. You go about your life and the interview does not do much of anything to add to the equation.

Can You Ask for the Questions in Advance?

People ask this all the time. The answer is almost always *no*. Some journalists feel it infringes on their integrity to give away the questions. Some don't want to reveal exactly what they plan to say and do. The real answer is that most do not know the exact questions in advance.

But here is what will help. Below is pretty much every question you will ever get asked in an interview:

WHO, WHAT, WHEN, WHERE, WHY, HOW

Essentially the famous 5W's of journalism will be asked of you.

Examples:

The 5 W's in action/questions you might get asked:

Who would this be for?
What are the uses?
When is the right time to use it?
Where is it being used?

Why did you write this book / want to release this product?
How can we benefit from having it?

Practice with these **Most Basic Questions.** This will ready you for almost everything that comes up. Use your other answer techniques for the more challenging questions.

Know the Game

Is this an informational interview? Is this a slam interview? *(one where they are out to get you)* Will they bring up that legal issue or bankruptcy from the past?

Know the game. Be prepared for it and be ready to win. Take the interview where you need it to go.

Control the Interview

Don't be bullied. You are not a child in a classroom. This is a media interview. You have control over what comes out of your mouth.

Paint the picture for them. If we are talking about cruelty to animals, tell us what the specifics are. If we are talking about sweet children helping the elderly, give us specifics. When people can *see* the idea, they can *feel* it. If you can get them to see and feel your point of view, you've won them over.

Freestyle Interviews

I mentioned "Freestyle" interviews in the last section. These are interviews where it is less about having the perfect, pre-planned messages in each answer, and more about being the expert or showing off your brand.

Let's build on that...

Now that you have the Answer System, you can use the techniques to take control of the interview. You can use them to guide the interview in the directions you want to go.

What to Worry About

Focus on your own preparation. Prepare by using the techniques discussed in this book so far. That is where your worry focus should be.

What NOT to Worry About

Focusing or *worrying* about every possible question you could get asked is an impossible task. Use your new Answer System!

How do you know you'll be able to use the *Answer System* in a real interview? Practice! And make sure you practice with a video recording device.

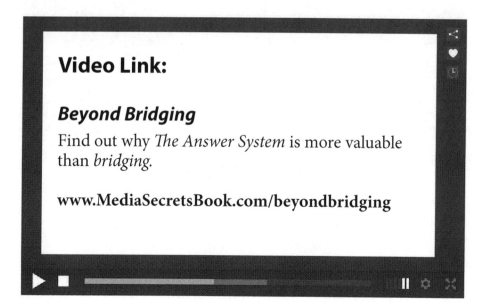

Video Link:

Beyond Bridging

Find out why *The Answer System* is more valuable than *bridging*.

www.MediaSecretsBook.com/beyondbridging

THE SOUND BITE QUOTE SYSTEM
Secrets to Creating Irresistible Answers the Media Loves and Uses

> *"Destiny is a name often given in retrospect to choices that had dramatic consequences."*
> **—J.K. ROWLING**

What Is a Sound Bite?

It's— that short answer the media uses from your interview.

Traditionally, it is that one, bite-sized, portion of "sound" taken from the larger body of what you said. You've seen them as the **clips** used in TV news packages. In print, of course, they are called **quotes**. Sometimes, especially in the case of print media, they commonly highlight something important that was said and enlarge it on the page (referred to as a **call-out**.)

Why Sound Bites Matter

Creating memorable sound bites is another way to **guide** (i.e. take control!) of the interview process. When you create an irresistible quote (or quotes), you have the most control over the answers answers/quotes that the reporter chooses.

This is a learned skill. Again, these are answers that are *within* the paragraphs you speak.

In a chat style interview, like you'd see on a morning show or cable news show, these phrases make your segment *pop*. They make you seem more polished, and add *sizzle* to what you're saying. , AND, if you come across that way, **you'll get asked back**.

The Sound Bite Quote System: Secret Techniques for Creating Irresistible Quotes

1. Absolutes
2. Facts
3. Examples
4. Action Words
5. Shocking
6. Predictions
7. Emotion
8. Conflict Quotes
9. Clichés or a *play* on a cliché
10. Triple Play
11. Rhetorical Questions
12. Analogies
13. Humor
14. Pop Culture References

The preceding 14 techniques, when included with the messages you have crafted, will turn those messages into SOUND BITES.

1. *Absolutes*

The media likes people who give answers that are *absolutes*. Get specific when speaking! Here are some absolutes:

"Our product is for ALL homeowners." Notice the word *all*. This person is speaking in absolutes.

Here's another: *"We can't be beat!"* or *"We will stop at nothing to get the job done!"* These are all absolutes.

Anytime you can speak in a way that is not wishy-washy, that is focused, it will work as a sound bite. **The media appreciates people who take a position and stand by it.**

2. Facts

Reporters and journalists speak to sources—that's YOU! You provide information or facts for them to use in their story. This is the substance or the examples they are looking for. It is an important part of their story, and you are providing it.

Examples:

"44% of people in this company only last two years."

"The concert will take place on the 12th of April."

"Avocados are one of the world's healthiest foods. They are an excellent source of fiber, folic and some of your most important vitamins."

3. Examples

Examples further solidify a point. This helps journalists and their audiences to best understand what you are talking about. Stories, anecdotes, and case studies work well here.

Some Examples:

Instead of just saying, "It was difficult to see," an animal welfare representative might expand and give this quote:

"When our animal rescue crew showed up, we found a small dog cowering in the corner. He was dirty and tired, and signs of abuse and neglect were rampant."

Instead of a school official saying "Our kids are great," they might include this example:

"We have one of the highest student volunteer rates in the state—as compared to other schools—one in three students finds a way to give back."

4. Action Words

Resume experts often agree that *action words* punch up your resume and help you stand out. The same goes for creating **quotable quotes.**

Here are some phrases (some answers) with action words:

"They pushed the law through."
Notice the word **pushed.**

"My client lost all the weight." **Lost**
"Follow the money." **Follow**
"Kick him out of that job!" **Kick**
"We'll be watching that company." **Watching**

Notice how the action words make those sentences feel more compelling.

5. *Shocking* Answers

Say something that is shocking or surprising. The media will like it and often quote you saying it.

Examples:

Say you had a weight-loss book, and you gave this answer:
"You can eat fast food AND lose 20 pounds—at the same time!"

Is that shocking? Yes, definitely. Here is a financial example:

"You can triple your income with $12 a week!"

"Our former boss admitted that he was clueless on the issues."

These are all examples that would get a reporter's attention.

6. *Predictions*

If you make predictions, journalists and media folks love it. They would rather someone else, an expert, give this opinion and make a prediction for the future. Predictions are very quotable.

Examples:

"Mark my words. A year from now this company will be out of business. This will catch up to her."

"I see this stock doubling over the next year."

"This person will be the new star of our industry."

"This politician is done. You can't say these things in public and expect to keep your job."

7. *Emotion*

Emotion is a key factor in the sales world. We connect, and/or make buying decisions, based on how something feels. This translates on the sound bite side. Reporters and audiences connect with answers that show how someone *felt*.

Here are a few quotes that have emotion embedded in them:

"I regret the choices that I've made, but I'm grateful for where I am today (because of them)."

Notice **regret** and **gratefulness**. It's emotion, and it makes the answer come alive.

"I was saddened to hear the news about this company going out of business."

Saddened.

"We couldn't be happier for the winning team."

Happier.

For those of you who are actually selling something during an interview—**pay close attention here.** We want to use sales triggers to not just *sell* our quote or answer, **but to drive people toward our point of view.** If you can tap into emotion, even when selling ideas, you are on the right track and a step closer to *converting interviews ...* into sales, web traffic and sign-ups.

Sound Bites make the interview pop and help you to sound like a media star!

8. Conflict Quotes

When I began my career as a TV producer, I remember one conversation, during a job interview, I will never forget. This high level, Executive Producer, asked me "What is drama?" I remember stammering around trying to explain that it was something *serious* or *compelling*. He was able to describe it in one word. **Conflict.** He explained that all stories, just like in literature, must have a problem or conflict. This made them more interesting. Later on I realized that *conflict* is one of the **14 core elements** for creating an irresistible quote.

Examples:

"We will expose the members of the council for the liars that they are!"

Alright, that's certainly an attack.

"That statement is shear lunacy!"

"People who hold those views are living in the stone ages."

9. Clichés

Clichés, believe it or not, are irresistible to the media. For this technique you can attach a cliché to one of your messages. Or, you can use a play on a cliché.

Examples:

"The bottom line is . . . [insert one of your messages]."

"Look, at the end of the day . . . [make your statement]."

You embed your message within the cliché. Doing so will dramatically increase the chance of getting that message out into the media.

Here are a few more:

*"We know our team can win, and **you can bet on it!**"*

*"Well, when it comes to knowing this, **time will tell.**"*

*"That is certainly the **name of the game.**" That organization has hit some **road blocks, but luckily it looks like there's a light at the end of the tunnel.**"*

All of these answers had a cliché attached to it. I want you to experiment with taking one of these clichés, or a different one, and attach it to one of your messages. See how it sounds. See if it jumps off the page and is attention-grabbing. Obviously, you ultimately need to be comfortable with any sound bites you decide to use with the media, and use only the ones you like most that you feel work for you.

Here's a last one, which is a play on a cliché:

"We found ourselves caught between a rock and a good place!"

This is a play on the cliché "Between a rock and a hard place." These are just as quotable and find their ways into stories every day.

10. *The Triple Play*

It is sometimes called "The rule of three." It's a writing principle that says we, as people, like stories, jokes and many other things in life to come in a group of three. We often like our information in neat packets of three. This is true for sound bites as well.

The idea here is simple—give three items in an answer.

Examples:

"We need endurance. We need strength. And we need persistence."

Notice there are three elements—endurance, strength and persistence.

"It's something that we want to do. Something we need to do. Something we have to do."

For whatever reason, the world loves threes. This technique works.

"They were evacuating men, women, and children."

The triple play can be irresistible to reporters, editors and producers.

(See that—just thought I'd include three groups to see if you were paying attention.)

11. *Rhetorical Questions*

Why are rhetorical questions useful when giving an interview? Because you get to ask your own questions and answer it too! Talk about control!

Examples:

Plus, it's a *Sound Bite Quote* technique.

"Is this the best plan for our country? You bet it is."

"Should we change our ways to change the environment? Absolutely."

"Are people better off with more fiber in their food? They are, and this change to our recipe is the right thing to do."

You want to be careful not to do this too many times during the interview. Of course, overuse would sound silly. Consider creating a couple of sound bites that use this element.

12. *Analogies*

An analogy is a literary device that helps to establish a relationship based on similarities between two concepts or ideas—saying *this* is like *that*. It is a technique that is also very quotable.

Examples:

"Those hungry athletes were like a pack of wolves."

"That politician was like a fish out of water in that debate."

I often use an analogy when I'm talking about media training workshops: "Learning media training skills is like learning to ride a bicycle. You can't just talk about it or read about it. You have to get up and try it out. Without practice, you will likely fall down."

13. *Humor*

Humor quotes can be very effective, but make sure you only use humor if it is appropriate and you feel comfortable with it.

Here's a quote from Mahatma Gandhi (he was speaking to reporters), *"I believe in equality for everyone except reporters and photographers."* There's some obvious humor there. And it got quoted, AND is still out there—floating around (many years after the actual interview).

Here's one from Mark Twain: *"Sometimes I wonder whether the world is being run by smart people who are putting us on or by imbeciles who really mean it."*

Here's another famous one by Yogi Berra: *"You wouldn't have won if we'd beaten you."*

If you have very serious topic, however, you should probably stay away from humor, unless you are very adept at using it to lighten the air of a heavy moment.

14. *Pop Culture References*

Pop culture references make a story sound hipper or relevant. It is an effective sound bite technique.

Examples:

"He has a fashion sense like Ronald McDonald."

"He was dancing around that issue like he was Britney Spears at the Super Bowl."

"People can wait around all they like, but he's not coming back. Elvis has left the building."

Here's a play on the famous Franklin Delano Roosevelt line, "The only thing we have to fear is fear itself." *The only thing we have to fear is my opponent!"* You can imagine that in a political debate. You might also notice that it has a little bit of humor, and is a conflict quote— there are a few different elements happening at the same time. And, while you only need to use one of the techniques when enhancing one of your messages, if you use more than one, they can become even more **powerful**.

If, after reading the 14 techniques, you are still in doubt around whether or not this system really works, go to today's newspaper—no matter where you are located. (The online version is fine for this exercise.) Look through the sections. Find places where people are quoted—where you see their answers in quotes. **You will see that these quotes match the elements I am highlighting here.** This system works, and using it will get you quoted in the media.

Do Other Sound Bite Techniques Exist?

Often I get asked, "Aren't there other sound bite creation strategies and techniques?" The answer is yes. Others include using an attractive quote or a clever alliteration or rhyme.

Example:

"If it doesn't fit, you must acquit."

These are not included in the core 14 because they are too difficult to create from scratch. Therefore, stick to the techniques in this chapter, and you'll be able to quickly and easily create sounds bites that will help you **stand out** and take **control**.

Putting It All Together

So, with the *Message, Answer, and Sound Bite Systems,* you have the core systems to be to be better prepared for an interview. Here is how you would do it more quickly…

Sit down and think to yourself: *What is the topic of discussion? What is the title of this interview?* Write out those media messages, divide them into three categories. Then add some sound bites. Also, using those three categories, take a quick look at your Answer System and practice in a much more focused way (on video).

Now go out and use these techniques in actual interviews, and send me a message to let me know how it went! (www.MediaSecretsBook.com/sendmessage)

Video Link:

Sound Bites

Learn about the importance of using sound bites in interviews.

www.MediaSecretsBook.com/soundbites

6

YOUR SECRET CONTROL
TECHNIQUES

*"It's ok to have your eggs in one basket as long as
you control what happens to that basket."*
—ELON MUSK

In the "Pitching" Stage

Is it possible to have more control in an interview when you haven't even secured the actual interview? Yes! Utilize the following techniques and you will start shaping the interview even before they say yes. Once they do decide to move forward with the interview, they will use information from *your pitch* when putting your interview or segment together. So, your pitch is the way to control the pre-interview process!

Headlines. Create a headline (like a newspaper headline) in your pitch email or press release. If it is really great, chances are, the media will use it in their story.

Examples:

"Now You Can Lose Weight and Eat Fast Food!"

"The 5 Best Ways to Beat Cold and Flu"

"Is it Time for Dogs to Have a Social Network of Their Own?"

Bullet points / Point of view. In your pitch email, include a list of bullet points on **what you might actually say.** The media will use these to help formulate their questions (especially if you have something good to say). Without these, your interviewer will have to ask a series of "discovery" questions just to get you to uncover something interesting. But, if you give them a list, the interviewer can lead you toward what works for both of you.

In print (and this has been my experience), some reporters will either get you to repeat the quote from your email/release, or just print the one they liked from the release. *Talk about control!*

"Sample Q & A." Include, in your press materials or press email, a section called "Sample Q&A." This gives the media a sense of what you might say. Do not, however, call it "Suggested Q & A." That sounds like you are trying to force your answers on them. A "sample" just gives them ideas they can try. Often, they will ask you many of the questions from that section. Why? Because you made their life easier.

Include Rhetorical Questions. You can use these in press releases/emails as well as interviews. It forces the interviewer to follow up on what you just said.

Example:

"How much does your family history play into your ability to lose weight?" As it turns out, it plays a bigger role than you'd think."

You have more control over interviews than you realize.

During the Interview

Lead the interviewer. This is a technique where you lead the interviewer toward something you really want to discuss. While answering one question, bring up another idea at the end of what you've said.

Example:

"… and those are the main numbers that came out today, but what people are really wondering is how this will affect the economy."

or

"This was a surprise, but, there was an even bigger shocker that we stumbled upon."

In both situations, the interviewer would likely ask a follow-up question to the information you just lead them toward.

Rhetorical questions. You've seen rhetorical questions show up in the *Answer System*, the *Sound Bite/Quote System*, and now this chapter— *Control Techniques.*

Rhetorical Questions are also great during the interview because they give you more control! You get to ask your own question and answer it too!

Example:

"Look, was this a bad idea from Congress? Absolutely. It all started when . . . "

And I'll tell you why. This is a great phrase that I stumbled on one day during an interview. You can add it after any of your statements (that you make during an interview) that you'd like to talk more about.

Examples:

"Smiling can extend your life by 10 years, and I'll tell you why ..."

"Eating broccoli will make your teeth whiter, and I'll tell you why..."

"Drinking cold water will speed up your metabolism, and I'll tell you why..."

The interviewer is along for the ride on this one. Just make sure you don't use this technique for every answer.

Plug without plugging (planting seeds). With this technique, you are half mentioning something that sends a signal to the audience.

Here are a few phrases authors might use:

"That's right Tom. In fact, I dedicated a whole chapter to that. ...and what I found was ..."

"When I was researching the book, I discovered something pretty surprising. I learned that ..."

"As an author, I find I planned to go down one path, yet ended up on another. What happened next was ..."

In all three of these examples, the author planted seeds in the mind of the audience that there is a book. In addition, for television, it is a cue to the control room to put the book cover on the screen or to put up the author's name and book title. All are win-wins for you. This—*half mentioning*—also translates to driving attention toward your business or product.

A New Take on PLUGing

Traditionally, the plug is the product mention by the interviewer or interviewee. This can be your website, company, book, etc.

The old idea of plugging something meant to *plug* or force your product mention into the conversation—I have a new take. Let's look at the word plug as an acronym. **P.L.U.G.** can now stand for:

*P*ROPERLY
*L*EVERAGE
*U*R (YOUR)
*G*IFT.

When you think about the idea of a **gift,** you are giving something of value. You can mention your website, but mention the benefit of going there. **This way,** *plugging* **feels good** and not overly self-promotional.

Another good plug is giving away a free item to the audience. This can be physical or electronic. Ideally, they have to go to your website and opt-in. You will not only make a great impression, but also make the outlet you are appearing on/in look good in the process—another win-win!

This *P.L.U.G.* should happen about three quarters of the way into the interview. It should not be "By the way, buy my book—here's my website." Using the media is a two-way street—not just a vehicle to promote yourself, your idea, or hawk your product! You must give value by providing interesting and important information during the conversation.

To do it right, you must create, in advance, an authentic *P.L.U.G.* that includes a **call to action**. The very best way to *P.L.U.G.* effectively is by offering something for free. Once you mention that there's something free, you can also mention that they can buy your item there or at places where books are sold. You can also direct them to go to your website, which is yet another great opportunity for them to get to know what you are all about.

Video Link:

Leverage With Opt-Ins

Need an easy way to create online opt-ins and pages? Watch the video on Easy Opt-ins

www.MediaSecretsBook.com/optins

SECRETS FOR LOOKING AND SOUNDING YOUR BEST
Your Outer Message (Body Language & Voice)

*"Style is very personal. It has nothing to do with fashion.
Fashion is over quickly. Style is forever."*
—RALPH LAUREN

Most media trainers **start** with body language. The truth is, if you don't have your messages down, or something valuable to contribute, body language won't matter. Getting this part right will, however, help you feel better ... which is an important part of the process.

If I were to **BOTTOM LINE** it, the **biggest issues** I see are: *Low Energy* and *Lack of body movement*.

If you can tackle these, you practically have this part taken care of.

Energy Level

Low energy = people who sound like they are less than happy to be part of the interview. If you record yourself, you'll notice that it often sounds more *low-key* than it felt.

The fix is to notice it and add more energy to the next practice or interview. To get people to have better energy during interviews, I have them try this...

Exercise:

I tell people to think of the word **PASSION**. If I were to ask you "why are you passionate about what you do?"

Chances are, you'd light up and start listing all the reasons. When *lit up* like this, you are often *in the zone*, showing full passion and exhibiting great energy.

How will you know if it is perfect or not?

Video record a mock interview. You'll know, in the first 15 seconds, if it's working or not. Often, especially on video, you have to add some extra energy for it to look just right.

Another interesting exercise is to practice one interview *"going over-the-top"* with your energy. I often do this with people who have trouble *being extroverted*. Next, play back the video to see what it looks and sounds like. What we find is, what they think is "over-the-top" tends to be just right for the rest of this.

If you're not passionate about your topic, no one else will be.

Locking down body language is something else I often see. . . This means standing, stiff as a board, hands frozen at your side or glued to the inside of your pockets. Not only does it affect your energy, it just looks unnatural and reduces you to a "talking head."

The following body language tips will help you to match your messages with your image.

Body Language

Entire books have been written on this topic, and this book aims to give you just what you *NEED* to know in order to do a great interview.

The goal is for you to *LOOK as NATURAL* as possible. Watch people on television. Watch people in daily life. You will notice that:

> ➤ They move their *heads* conversationally
> ➤ They move their *bodies* slightly
> ➤ They move their *hands* naturally

Just making sure you are moving these three areas will help you *look*, and then *feel* better during interviews.

Hands—What You Need to Know

People often ask me if they should have specific gestures to go along with special phrases. I think this is silly and a waste of time. Half the battle is getting people to use their hands at all. You want the gestures to be natural and match what you are saying. Video tape yourself and you'll see if you use "natural" gestures or have artificial ones.

Use your hands. Bring them up to the middle of your chest so it can be seen on camera.

Standing-up interviews

You want your hands to be seen in the camera shot. Usually the camera frames you in a mid-shot, around the waste. So, for this you'll have to bend your arms at the elbows and raise them 90 degrees. They are now in the shot. Now speak naturally and move your hands like you would in normal conversation.

So far, this technique is fine as long as you are talking, but what do you do with your hands while you are listening to questions? For this, you place one hand over the other, with the finger tips touching the palm or other finger tips on the other hand.

Why do this? Because it gives you something to do other than locking down your hands as a clasp or putting them in your pockets. As soon as the interviewer finishes their question, you move your hands, along with your words, in a natural conversational way.

Also, having your feet side by side could accentuate any unintended rocking. Instead, put one foot forward and anchor, rest, on your back leg. You will find that this often eliminates any potential rocking.

Sitting-down interviews

If you have a table in front of you, you can rest your forearms on the end of the table. This way they are out and about, not locked down. Gesture naturally when you are speaking. *(Note: Placing them under the table will make you look like a child.)*

If there is no table in front of you and people can see most of your body, rest your hands on your thighs or knees when you are not talking. When answering questions, lift them up and gesture in the mid-region of your chest so the camera can see the movement. Again, gesture as you would in normal conversation. Don't try to create anything that looks unnatural.

Avoid resting your arms on armrests. You will notice that all hand gestures seem to stop.

Don't spin around if you have a spinning chair. Seems like it goes without saying, but people fidget. Try to stay in one place.

Crossing your legs during interviews is not advised because it pushes your upper body back in your chair. It could make you look overconfident or arrogant. It also can make you look heavier on camera.

Instead, cross one foot on your ankle. If you are wearing a skirt, you can put your knees and feet together with your feet just off to the side.

Tilt forward on your pelvis 15 degrees so you can avoid what is on the next page. . . .

The Camera Adds 10 Pounds— and How to Make it STOP!

As the old joke goes, "How many cameras did they have on me???"

Get rid of the "camera adds 10 pounds" problem.
Lean forward 15%.

Why Does This Happen Exactly?

3D to 2D. Part of the problem stems from the fact that you are taking a three-dimensional object and showing it on a two-dimensional surface.

Bad lighting. Depending on the lighting, it is difficult for the camera to capture depth. Straight-on lighting can have a flattening effect.

Shadows. Shadows can often make you look larger. Shadows from a camera flash or an ill-placed light can add extra shape to one's form.

Wide angle lenses. Lenses with a short focal length could make a person appear wider.

Wearing white. Some think this can make you look larger. This does make logical sense if you understand that someone dressed in all-white would certainly look the biggest and brightest on the screen.

Wearing black. Since black absorbs more light, it makes it difficult to see the definition between say your arms and your torso. If they blend together (lighting is a factor here, too), then you may just look like a blob on screen.

Secrets to NOT Having the Camera Add 10 Pounds

1. *What is closest to the camera is the largest!* In sitting interviews, if you are sitting up against the back of your chair, your stomach is closest to the camera and your head is slightly further away. This will make your stomach look larger and your head smaller! To look amazing on-camera, *tilt forward on your pelvis about 15 degrees.* This will place your head closer to the camera than your belly. You will look trimmer and even more engaging because you look like you are on the edge of your seat.

2. *Positioning.* For standing interviews, turn *slightly to the side* with one foot in front of the other towards the camera. If you turn too much, it will look like you are trying to take a "fashion runway photograph." This slight angle will help you look slimmer and give you a slight edge.

3. *Clothing.* Take the eyes off the *belly region.* If you are wearing a suit, button the buttons. An open jacket will draw attention to that area of your torso. Buttoning will bring people's eyes away from the trouble zones.

4. *Shapewear or compression clothing.* Women have been fortunate to get extra help from *Spanks* (and other similar brands). They squeeze everything in. It can help many people to have a more slimming look. Men, don't feel left out. Now, you too, can cinch in that gut! They make undergarment products like this for men, as well.

5. *Camera angles.* This is something you only have control over if you are doing your own production (same goes for lighting). In the age of video conferencing and Skype video interviews, you want to position the camera slightly above the eye line. This will cause you to look up slightly and stretch out the chin. A camera angled lower will cause even the thinnest person to look "multi-chinned."

> The bottom line on this matter is simply this: for sitting interviews, tilt 15 degrees forward on your pelvis. For standing interviews, button your jacket. Have your body turned slightly to the side, not head on.

BODY LANGUAGE ISSUES

Person stands with hands glued to their sides.
Result: looks strange, and ends up looking like they are stiff as a needle.

Person stands with hands in pockets.
Result: looks way too relaxed, and will likely leave their hands that way during the entire interview—reducing them to a bobbing head.

Person stands with hands behind their back.
Result: appears like someone with no arms or hands. What's worse is they look like they are handcuffed. That doesn't instill confidence.

Person pointing.
Result: Being perceived as rude. If you do it here or there, it's not the end of the world but you should be conscious of this. A quick fix: Try extending your hand, palm up, as a new way to point. Using your hands instead of pointing fingers is less aggressive way to point.

Person folding their arms.
Result: appears angry. We've all heard that crossing one's arms looks like you are angry and places a barrier between you and someone else. It could make you appear to be on the defensive and guarded—not exactly the message you want to give off. I rarely see people do this in interviews, but it is worth mentioning.

Move Your Head and Torso

Just make sure you are not *unconsciously* locking your head and torso down. The best way to catch/prevent this is to record yourself and then watch the playback. As you are watching, notice if **only** your face and mouth is moving (this means you are locking your head and torso). Allow these areas to be loose. If you are moving them, along with your hands, you'll look like a pro. The video is a key ingredient in knowing where you stand.

I have trained some TV anchors who noticed, while practicing, that their heads moved like "Bobbleheads." The reason was that they were ONLY moving their heads. They were able to make corrections on the very next practice and quickly improve their style.

Using Your Voice

What is the goal?

You want to sound interesting and authoritative.

Sounding Interesting. Have good energy in your voice. That's where your passion shows. Use pauses. Hit certain words harder for emphasis. Add inflection so you can focus the audience in on the words that matter most.

Being Authoritative

Say what you mean and mean what you say. Speak with authority.

1. If you have plenty of "ums," "ahs" or other verbal fillers, you won't sound like much of an authority on what you are speaking about. If you think this is something you need to work on—i.e. you've heard yourself, on a recording, using one of these verbal fillers. For example, uttering *Um, Ah, Like, You Know, etc.*—this technique that will help:

   First, get upset. Realize that this is not making you sound interesting or smart. Being upset, feeling some pain when you think about this is good, and part of the solution. One of the biggest motivators toward change is "trying to avoid pain." I want you to think about the pain associated with not fixing this issue. Are you feeling it? Good. Now take action.

2. Action: Record yourself with an audio program that not only captures your sound, but shows a visual of your sound waves on the screen. *Audacity* is a great (and free) product available on the Internet. When you play back your recording, you will notice how different the *ums* and *ahs* look visually.

3. Next, highlight and delete the *ums* and *ahs* just like you would with words you were deleting in a word processing program.

4. Play back the *fixed* audio recording. You will be shocked at how much different and more authoritative you sound.

HELP! My Voice Sounds Different on Recordings

It sounds different because you are hearing the sound differently. "When you speak, the vocal folds in your throat vibrate, which causes your skin, skull and oral cavities to also vibrate—and we perceive this as sound." If you mix those vibrations with sound waves going from your mouth to your eardrum, it tends to give the voice a deeper tone.

This is a sound we are used to, and one that nobody else hears! However, through a recording device, you only hear the sounds going through the air. The sounds we're used to hearing have a lower frequency due to those bone vibrations. The recording does not sound as full and rich as we are used to.

It makes it hard to accept that this is our voice. Some say they sound weak or just strange. This supports the idea that we're hearing less of the low frequency and more of the high.

While it may be jarring to hear this slightly different version of your voice, it is just something you have to accept . . . and move on.

One caveat: over the years, I have had a very small handful of clients who had either a very high or low pitched voice. This, along with accents, requires exercises given to you by a speech therapist or speech pathologist. If you don't think you are at one of the extremes, try not to be too hard on yourself.

Standing Up

Standing up during a phone interview or when recording your voice can help it to sound fuller and more interesting. Why? Standing up opens your breathing vs sitting down where your chest is compressed. It makes it easier to take deeper breaths. You will likely use more of your body language, which will add more emphasis to your words.

Tip: Using your body language will actually improve the sound of your voice. If you are doing an interview over the phone, don't lie in bed or sit slumped in a chair. Get up and move around. A recording will prove there's a difference.

Low Talkers/Loud Talkers

Either extreme can be a problem. If you are a *low* (volume) *talker*, you might come across as weak or as someone who is timid in asserting your views. The fix? Pretend the interviewer is actually 5 to 10 feet further away from you. Pick an object that is *that* distance away and practice throwing your voice to it. This will help you to bring your volume up and look more like an authority.

Are you too loud? You don't want to come across as *too* dominating. Look for opportunities throughout the day to test out your midrange volume. Record/listen to yourself more often, so you can hear what others are experiencing.

Protect Your Voice

As singers know, your voice is an instrument. There are a few things you can do to keep it protected:

- ➢ Avoid smoking, alcohol, coffee and screaming before an interview. They can wear your voice down.
- ➢ Do your best to get extra rest the night before you plan to speak.
- ➢ Do drink plenty of water so you and your vocal chords are well hydrated.
- ➢ Speaking for long periods of time can *tire* your voice. If you are not used to this (speaking for long periods), do your best to pace yourself. Using a microphone can also help you preserve your voice.
- ➢ Avoid medications or foods that create excess mucous.

Turn Your Biggest Negative Into a Positive

I've done this with many clients over the years. Many feel it's their voice, their looks, their age or a whole host of other possible troubles. I say "Turn Your Biggest Negative (what you think it is) Into a Positive."

Example:

I was coaching a financial advisor a few years ago. Let's call him, Tom. Tom was a tall, stocky gentleman, likely in his sixties, with gray hair and glasses. His voice was rough and gravely. When I heard him speak in front of the group, I could tell that it was getting in the way of his messages and what he was trying to communicate.

After having him listen to a recording of himself, I asked him what feedback he had heard about his voice over the years. He said people found it intimidating. I told him that we could take what he thought was his biggest negative and *create new meaning.*

After hearing Tom for 5 or 10 minutes, I realized that he reminded me of a basketball coach. These coaches are tough, but fair, and you really want their advice. I shared that with him and he lit up. I told him that I was going to call him Coach Tom, the financial coach, for the rest of the day. He told me he loved it and worked it into his branding.

Still Have Issues With Your voice?

There are plenty of other nuanced voice issues that could be brought up. If you still feel you need help in this area, do some more research or seek out a professional who can help.

EYE CONTACT

Where Should You Look?

In most cases, you should make and keep eye contact with your interviewer. Ignore the camera, lights, producers, etc. Focus on talking to the real person interviewing you, using their reactions to connect in a more natural conversational way.

If you are doing an interview via satellite, video conference, or Skype, you should look directly into the camera. This may feel strange or odd. The trick is to pretend that there is a person's face reacting to everything you say. Ideally, that *pretend* person is enjoying everything you are saying. This takes a little practice. It is very important to look at the camera in these circumstances. If you don't, it will look like you are ignoring or not respecting the host or audience. You may seem disconnected or distracted, too.

If you are doing an interview over the phone, either for print or radio, you should be looking at your notes. Don't read emails or surf the web. In fact, print out your notes. If they are on your computer, the screen saver will likely come on at the worst moment. Print out your Message Grid and keep that *Road Map* in front of you.

The TV Smile

Smile or No Smile? What is the protocol?

A little common sense helps as you decide what is best for your interview. If you are talking about a serious topic, it's okay to look serious. If you have a lighter topic, it's okay to smile.

BUT . . .

During questions or introductions, you don't want to look stiff and boring. This is where you definitely want to use the "TV Smile."

To do this, you bring the sides of your mouth up just slightly. You might even feel it in your cheeks up by your eyes.

If you think sitting there expressionless is no problem, you haven't seen yourself doing it. TV will make it look like you are unhappy to be there, bored, angry, or possibly scared.

Is that the message you're going for?

If not, practice using the TV Smile and notice how much more interesting and confident you look.

BODY LANGUAGE AND VOICE

Other Common Problems

While I have covered the most important areas, a few other problems pop up from time to time. These are not as common, but deserve mention as well. Here are some problematic situations and possible solutions:

Head tilting too much. Some people watch the playback of their video and feel that their head is tilting too much to the side. When I ask others in the session if they noticed it, few did, or were even bothered by it, if it did occur. If YOU are bothered by nuances in your body language, notice it on your practice videos and adjust during your next practice interview.

Blinking too much. This is a sign of nervousness. Practicing will help eliminate more of that "fear of the unknown" and will help a great deal. Good news though, most people won't even notice your eye movements.

Some experts say people who are lying blink excessively. The cure for *that* is *not lying*.

Dry mouth. Stay hydrated and drink water or other sugar free juices *prior* to the interview. If you are thirsty, you are already dehydrated, so get plenty to drink when you wake up that morning and prior to the interview. You can have water with you during the interview, but try your best not to be drinking during the interview itself. It takes time away from you being able to deliver your messages, and can be distracting in an interview. Reducing your intake of caffeine could help, too, because beverages with caffeine can be dehydrating.

I know that last point is tough for many who rely on coffee to get started in the morning. Here's a workaround. Leave a tall glass of water next to your bed before going to sleep. When you wake up, drink the whole thing. Notice how your system reacts. It can feel like a rush of energy through your metabolism. You end up starting your day hydrated and ready to take on the world. Try it!

Other remedies… Avoid alcohol, even small amounts found in items like mouthwash could cause trouble if dry mouth is an issue for you. Chewing sugar-free gums or sucking on sugar-free candies can stimulate saliva production and thus prevent dry mouth. Just try not to do any of these things *during* the interview.

Strong accents. The big question here: does your accent get in the way of people understanding you? Or do you feel judged in some negative way (because of your accent)? Do people have trouble understanding you and often ask you to repeat what you are saying?

If you feel there are issues here, you must seek out a speech pathologist or accent reduction coach who can give you specific exercises to minimize issues and help people understand what you are saying.

Short term, *slowing down* can be a huge help.

Identifying and *annunciating* problem words can also make a difference.

Running out of air while speaking. When some people speak, they run out of air and find that they can't get any more words out. They feel embarrassed and have to gasp for more air, mid-sentence.

One big fix is taking in a nice, deep breath while the interviewer is asking you a question. Just make sure it is not obvious and can't be heard on a recording. Many news anchors will quietly fill with air as the stage manager counts them down from a commercial break into the show. They realize this is fuel for sounding great.

The real cause of this is nervousness. Practicing and doing your best to take as much of the "unknown" out of the interview equation will help you *feel* calmer and breathe normally.

MAKEUP

The big rule on TV makeup is this . . .

The audience shouldn't notice your makeup. If they can tell it's there, then it was applied incorrectly.

As I said earlier in the book, this is exactly the way I feel about media training techniques. If the audience notices techniques you are using, and are commenting about it, then you have applied them incorrectly. This will cause people to miss your messages, and possibly lose faith and trust in what you are saying.

It is also important to understand that no matter who you are or how perfect you might look, once you are under TV lights, makeup is needed so you will not be shiny, you will not look sick, faded, washed out, or wrinkly. Ideally, with the correct amount of makeup, you start to look more like you, or slightly better.

If you are doing a TV interview and the channel provides makeup, take it.

If you are doing a TV interview (or anything on camera) and they do not provide makeup, make sure you are prepared with some basic foundation or powder. You will look better and you will be happy you had it.

If You Don't Usually Wear Makeup

This applies to some women and most men.

If you do not usually wear makeup and are hesitant, know that not wearing makeup could get in the way of your messages. If you look tired, worn out, and not as good as your interviewer(s), something will seem off. If you want to look your best on TV, a little bit of makeup goes a long way.

Use this as an excuse to visit a store that specializes in makeup or your local department store's makeup counter. Even a large drugstore that has a makeup department will do. Tell the store's associate that you are doing some on-camera work and just want some basic foundation so you won't shine.

I went to the local drug store and had my wife pick one that matched my skin tone. It might also be helpful to go online to learn about different products and how to apply them correctly. Knowing how to apply some makeup is a must if you plan to be on-camera.

How To Quickly Improve Your Media Style

I don't mind sounding like a broken record because this is an important point. It is also a helpful technique for other topics brought up in this book, AND will help you look more comfortable on camera.

It's . . .

Using a Video Camera!

The Exercise

Practice doing a few 60-second interviews. Don't worry about making sure the content is perfect. Focus **all your energy** on making sure your body language and voice is where it should be.

If you wanted to learn a new dance, practice would be a key ingredient in your improvement. The same can be said for learning (and applying) best practices for looking your best on camera.

This is the exercise I use in live workshops. It is an amazing tool and one that you will benefit highly from.

What to Worry About

I've trained thousands of clients, and many of them share the same worry: is their body language working on camera. Here are the most important items you should be ~~worrying~~ thinking about:

FOCUS ON HAVING GOOD ENERGY.

Video Link:

On-Camera Makeup
Check out these video tutorials to help you look your best when on-camera.

www.MediaSecretsBook.com/makeup

Make sure you look natural and confident. As long as you look that way, people will believe it is true. Think back to experiences in your life where you acted the part and got credit for being that part. Use the *ACT IT and BECOME IT* technique.

Are there any glaring issues you are seeing during practice? Address them and make a conscious effort to change them. If there are minor ones, resolve to work on them—but don't obsess over it.

What NOT to Worry About

Don't put all your energies into worrying about having the *perfect* body language.

Don't worry if you *licked your lips* here or there. Many people worry about this. If you think your lips might be dry, go buy some lip balm and stay hydrated with a bottle of water—problem solved.

Maybe you like standing interviews over sitting, or the other way around. Be ready for both and be glad you are getting yourself and your messages into the story.

If you got the perfect messages you wanted into an interview, but used some body language here or there that was less than perfect, consider yourself a winner. Make the fixes next time, but consider yourself ahead of most people who have no control over their own answers.

THE MIND OF THE MEDIA
Secrets to What They're Thinking

*"Don't be intimidated by what you don't know.
That can be your greatest strength and ensure that you
do things differently from everyone else."*
—SARA BLAKELY, SPANX® FOUNDER

So what is going on inside the heads of the producers, bookers, writers, editors, reporters, etc.?

To work well with the media, and to have them want to interview you again in the future, you need to give them what *they* want. You must make their lives easy. You must become a resource for them. This goes for traditional media, as well as Internet journalists who might want to interview you for their blog or YouTube. In this chapter, we will get inside their heads.

Three Objectives to Keep in Mind

You must fulfill the needs of:

1. The Media Outlet/Entity
2. The Audience
3. You

Of course, the media are most concerned with the needs of the first two groups. If you can do a great job giving information that supports these two groups, they will want to promote you, your product, brand or business.

THE MEDIA OUTLET'S NEEDS—THE BREAKDOWN

TV

For Television, you might be contacted by a Producer with one of many titles. On the regional or national level, it is likely a *Booker* or *Segment Producer will contact you*. On the local level, it might be someone who wears many hats, and has many jobs/duties.

This person is looking for guests for *stories*. They might need *quotes*. They might need a guest who can talk for 2 to 5 minutes—possibly more.

What Don't They Want?
They want someone who:

➤ is interesting
➤ can give analysis or facts to support their story
➤ can appeal to or supply information to their demographic
➤ has something of value to share with their audience
➤ offers a *takeaway*—as a producer, we would consider the following: what can the audience take away from the segment? Did they learn something they didn't know before? For example, did the audience learn a new recipe? Get unique analysis on a topic? Or even a list of the top five ways to do something they could not do prior to hearing the information?

What are they thinking?
They are thinking:

➤ How can I complete the task in front of me without doing an inordinate amount of work?
➤ How can I choose someone to work with that makes me look good?
➤ Can I choose someone that will get me praise from my boss?
➤ Can this person get me better ratings or other positive audience attention?
➤ Will this person be helpful today?
➤ Could this person be helpful *to me* in the future?
➤ Will they be easy to reach?
➤ Can they be so easy to work with that they supply any information that helps me see the task through to completion?

Notice that many of these items fall under the category of "What's in it for me?" If you help them, and make their lives easier, they will want to help you—usually in the form of an on-air plug or promotion.

What don't they want?
They don't want someone who:

➢ Doesn't have much in the way of substance to add to the story.
➢ is self-promoting and cares more about their agenda.
➢ is a prima donna.
➢ is difficult to get a hold of or does not return their calls.
➢ they have to pry information out of or is long winded.
➢ is confusing.
➢ looks unkept or is in need of a major look update/makeover.
➢ Someone who might shine a negative spotlight on them or their organization.

Be attentive to the dos and don'ts above. Do your best to be easy and supportive.

Print

Usually print reporters are looking for quotes and experts who can give them relevant information for stories.

Many public relations representatives report to me that their client talked to a print reporter for an hour only to find that the client didn't end up in the piece. The reason for this is that the client never gave the reporter what they were looking for . . . QUOTES!!! Use your *Sound Bite System from Chapter 5.*

What do they want?
They want someone who can:

➢ tell them something interesting
➢ help the story
➢ advance the story
➢ offer value/give something their readers want or need
➢ someone who is easy to work with
➢ someone who can quickly get to the point

Reporters are often on a deadline. You must be accessible. If you can't answer your phone, offer a number for text message and reply quickly. This will benefit you long-term.

What don't they want?
They don't want someone who:

➢ is confusing.
➢ does not give them any new information.
➢ is demanding and want the story done their way.
➢ wants to see/approve the story before it is run.
➢ wants to see questions in advance.
➢ can't speak in quotable sound bites.

Radio

Radio shows might have you on for a few minutes, or they might have you on for an hour. For them, it's all about keeping their audience happy and tuned in.

What do they want?
They want someone who:

➢ understands their audience
➢ gives plenty of value to their listeners
➢ has something interesting or surprising to share on the air
➢ shows up (or calls in) on time
➢ calls in on a phone with a decent connection

Just like TV producers, radio producers want someone who can make their lives easier, supply relevant information, and make them look great in front of their audience and superiors.

As for the quality of your voice, unless you have an extreme problem (too high, too low, you stutter, thick accent, etc.) you should be fine. Refer to the Um/Ah exercise from the previous chapter if that is your issue. Verbal clutter like that will be more noticeable and amplified when others are only hearing your voice.

Note: Do your best to use a land line if you are calling in. Shoddy cell service won't cut it and will upset the producer, host, audience and everyone associated with the show. That will insure you don't get asked back. A clear land line will remedy this so you can focus on your part ... giving great information.

If you are forced to use a cell phone, make sure you have a clear connection, are not in a moving vehicle, and hope your wireless provider doesn't accidentally drop the call.

Also, be sure to disable *Call Waiting* (if you have this service), to prevent that annoying "click" or drop in audio, which would be a nuisance.

Internet Media

The information super highway, as it was once popularly called, IS still the "wild west" to some degree. Every day it evolves and citizen journalists have growing credibility. A *news and information* source can include bloggers, podcasters, *YouTubers*, E-zine publishers, micro-bloggers (think Twitter or Tumbler). Anyone with a smartphone can broadcast a message, video, or otherwise to everyone on the globe. This is not a group to take lightly. What shows up under your name or brand in a Google search is how many will view you. An article in USA Today might be side by side with a podcast where you let your guard down and talked like you would in private.

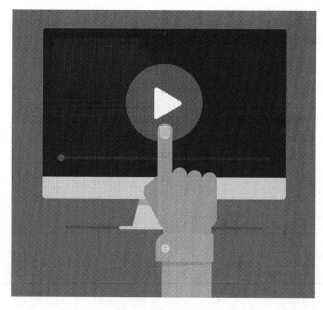

This group has all the same needs as traditional media, TV, print, and radio folks. Make them look good.

But…

They also have their own needs:

> ➤ They usually want to reach a larger audience than they already do. Can you offer to share the interview on your social media pages and with any of your followers? Can you share it with your email list or other marketing lists you might have?
> ➤ Is the content more than just interesting? **Is it sharable?** This is a big point for these people because it means more web traffic and eye balls. If more people see the story on their site, they can charge more for advertising, AND extend their reach and relevance. .
> ➤ **"Link Bait."** Do a quick web search for the phrase and you'll see that this group wants content that others want to link to. Do some research on the web to see what comes up for your topic. You might be able to give "suggested topic titles."
> ➤ Outbound Links. This group is happy to link to you so they can provide relevant content to their audience. It also helps them with search engine rankings.
> ➤ Original content. Because search engine rankings are important, they want content that has not been seen elsewhere. Original, first run content, especially in print, is important to them.

Note: This chapter has been assuming that you are doing positive interviews. If you are on the defense or dealing with crisis, see Chapter 9.

Who are these *online* media outlets?

There are a number of established *News & Information* Internet media outlets:

> ➤ The online version of every major TV network in the world. This includes ABC, NBC, CBS, FOX, CNN, MSNBC FOX News, BBC and so on.

➢ Every *local city* affiliate of ABC, NBC, CBS, FOX, WB, and The CW
➢ The Huffington Post
➢ Slate.com
➢ BusinessInsider.com
➢ Buzzfeed.com
➢ Vox.com
➢ vice.com
➢ Upworthy.com
➢ Medium.com

Of course, let's not forget these Internet power houses:

➢ YouTube
➢ Facebook
➢ Facebook Live
➢ Twitter
➢ LinkedIn
➢ Instagram
➢ Periscope
➢ Snapchat

What to Expect

These outlets have different needs. An established outlet might be looking to interview you via video. The Huffington Post often does this. They shoot in their TV studio and showcase videos with high production value. You'll want to prep like you would for any TV interview.

The polar opposite of this is an interview with someone who holds their smartphone in front of them, *selfie style*, while asking you questions. They may even use a selfie stick. This may take place at a conference or event. You often have little time to prepare. Think about what you want out of the interview and how you can best support those who will see it. Ask questions, prior to the interview, about their audience and what they'd like best from you. Weave in some sound bites and calls to action. Try to "P.L.U.G." ... give something away—(e.g. a free gift that drives the audience towards your website, your YouTube channel, etc.).

You might find that the *Internet journalist* wants to interview you over the phone or via Skype. Skype audio works well for many podcasts. Some will want to do a video interview with you via Skype and record it. Treat this like you would any other TV interview. Follow the techniques on TV interviews in this book.

A few more items to think about when being interviewed on video over Skype (or other video conferencing systems):

> ➢ *Lights.* Make sure you have proper lighting. Do a test run with a friend.
> ➢ *Camera.* Make sure your webcam works and looks good. You can do this during the same test.
> ➢ *Sound.* Make sure you have a microphone attached. iPhone headphones and their built in mic work very well for this if you don't have other equipment.
> ➢ *Background.* Make sure you have an interesting background. Seeing your refrigerator in the background or your cat walking through probably won't help unless it has something to do with your topic. Test out different locations in your home or office to see what looks best. Depth is your friend. If you can use a location that has plenty of depth it will be more interesting. If you prefer to sit in front of a curtain, do your best to make it interesting. I have a New York City backdrop that I often use when I need to quickly shoot a webcam interview.
> ➢ *Hands.* If you are sitting close to the camera, see what your hand gestures look like on the video. The closer the objects are, the larger they are. If your hands are right up against the camera, they will look giant and likely distracting.

This content will **live on for a long time** on the Internet. Do a good job. It might rank first when people search for your name.

If the outlet is not looking for something video or audio related, they might be looking to interview you for an article or have you write a guest blog. In either case, we are back to the main themes of this chapter: **Keep their audience in mind and give great information.**

If you have done right by the outlet, and helped make them look good, you can usually get them to link to your site. While traditional media sometimes gives you trouble about mentioning or plugging your site, Internet media folks know that links from their site to your (and in reverse) only help with search engine rankings—**win-win.** This is even true with traditional media outlets that have an Internet presence.

Can you satisfy everyone? Do your best to satisfy the needs of the three groups, and you'll be on the right track.

MEDIA
AUDIENCE
YOU

We always want:

➤ to give plenty of value
➤ to offer interesting content
➤ to look and sound interesting

CRISIS COMMUNICATION
Be Ready for Anything

"It takes twenty years to build a reputation and five minutes to ruin it."
—WARREN BUFFET

What Is a Crisis?

Crisis Communication is sometimes considered a subspecialty of public relations. This is when things go from being just a friendly interview to one where your brand or personal reputation is at stake.

I'm keeping this chapter short and sweet—Why?

To me, prepping for a crisis is about practicing, in advance, **before** a crisis strikes, by using the techniques discussed in this book or by having staff go through a media training program. These programs are designed around scenarios a particular company might face. Practicing, using the media training systems to deal with these, and having well-trained staff and spokespeople to handle a variety of media situations will definitely put you in the best position.

Some organizations wait until an actual crisis happens to start working on the plan. This is a bad idea. Different public relations firms and crisis management teams then come in, charge a premium, and you have to play catch-up. **Be smart: plan ahead.**

Top 10 Crisis Communication Strategies:

1. ***Don't Delay.*** Quickly get your top messages together.
2. ***Get Ahead of the Story.*** When crisis strikes, you need to react and be in control the story, or the media's version will own YOU. Be quick to jump out early with a statement, and/or have a spokesperson available, in order to get your voice out there as one of the first and main voices heard during the issue. This way the public will know that you are not scared, that you are very much involved, and that you are on top and in control of the situation. The media are story tellers. Jump in early so they'll tell YOUR version.
3. ***Any Plan Is Better Than No Plan.*** Figure out protocol, including what you will or will not talk about. Know who is speaking to the media and who isn't. Establish a chain of communication and command. Decide on times you'll be sharing some information with them.
4. ***OWN the Story.*** Continue to be the main voice advancing the narrative.
5. ***Control.*** For Q & A sessions with the media, let them know that you can only give answers to some questions and give a good reason. The reason could be because of the sensitivity of the situation or private or legal matters, etc.

Get ahead of the story before it gets ahead of you.

6. ***Clear Path of Access.*** Make sure the media feels connected and not "dodged" or avoided by you or your company. Decide on a phone number and email address that will be used for communication with the media. Make sure to monitor requests and respond … even if the response is *"We will be giving a statement and interviews at X time."*

7. ***Streamline*** your process for getting information out.

8. ***The Heart.*** Make sure your messages have some heart to them. Companies that show they have compassion, sympathy, or empathy usually get it in return from the public.

9. ***Solutions.*** Have a plan to fix the situation or to avoid a similar crisis in the future.

10. ***Share.*** Share that plan with the media, and do your best to make that the focus of the story.

Read the next two chapters on *Media Traps* and *Mistakes.* Many may feel that they are *crisis* strategies but are really strategies everyone should know about.

STAY AHEAD OF THE STORY WHEN POSSIBLE. PLAN IN ADVANCE . . . TRAIN IN ADVANCE.

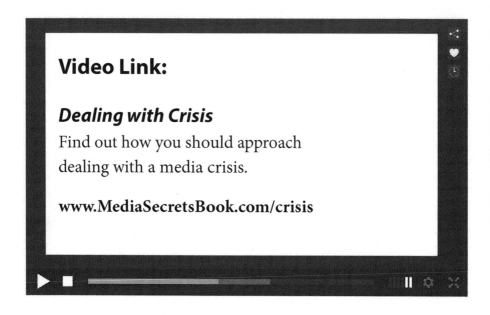

Video Link:

Dealing with Crisis

Find out how you should approach dealing with a media crisis.

www.MediaSecretsBook.com/crisis

MEDIA TRAPS

"Challenges have always made us better and stronger."
—MARK PARKER, NIKE CEO

One thing that keeps people up at night is the idea that reporters or journalists will try to trap them. This means different things to different people. "Trapping" could mean that they "put words in your mouth." It could be that they misrepresent, misquote or, portray you negatively. It could mean that they promised one type of interview and surprised you by asking questions you didn't want to answer.

All journalists are not "trying to get you." In fact, I would say that a majority are not out to get you. I would not broad-brush them in this manner. But, you need to consider a couple of things. One, are you defending a company experiencing a crisis, or representing a topic that is controversial? If so, you need to be prepared, with all of the systems in this book, and understand the common media traps. Two, are you speaking to the media about something fun and not controversial at all? For instance, if you are being interviewed about three ways people can exercise at their desk during the day, there is a far less chance that they are you going to trap, sabotage, or try to make you look bad in any way. They might ask silly or uniformed questions, but that is what your Answer System is for. In that scenario they might still voice some objections or concerns that they think their audience is thinking, but understand that you are there to offer information and value to their audience.

Here are some common situations that could be seen as *Traps*. Understand them so you do not have to feel like a victim.

You Are Quoted Repeating Something *They* Said

Sometimes journalists will ask that you repeat *their* question during an interview. For video or audio interviews that are being edited, this could help them if they are trying to edit themselves out. But, they can also put forward a false premise or something that you really don't want to say … and get you to say it. Protecting yourself should be your first goal.

Example:

Q: *"Isn't it true that a lot of people have lost faith in your company because the stock price has gone down?"*

In this situation, the person being interviewed might *mistakenly* respond:

A: *"Some people might have lost faith because our stock price went down, but what we have found is that this is a very small cross section of our loyal stockholders. In fact, most love us because…"*

The problem here is that the quote might show up as:

> *"Some people might have lost faith because*
> *our stock price went down."*
> **–BOB SMITH**
> *Soon to be Past CEO of XYZ Company*

Plus, Bob Smith might not really feel that anyone has "lost faith." The lesson here is **not to repeat** anything that you don't feel comfortable being quoted as saying. **Don't allow anyone to put words in your mouth!**

The Combative Interviewer

Ideally, familiarize yourself with this person's work and personality prior to the interview. This will help you get a sense of their style and know what to expect.

Go through the pros and cons of doing an interview with this person. Will they still allow you to get your point of view through? Will there be a price to pay by *not* doing this interview? Some news outlets will use an exterior shot of the person's office—who has declined the interview. They will then show that picture and tell their version of the story on their show or in print, while wondering what you have to hide (and projecting this sentiment onto their audience.)

Don't allow yourself to be swept up by their combative personality. Stand your ground. Keep your cool. Use the Answer System. Think of their questions as objections that you should be answering. The more you deal with their objections, and make your case, the more you'll have members of their audience on your side.

Tell them when you disagree with the premise they put forward and follow it with your premise and point of view.

Expressions

Be very aware of the expressions you have on your face (for TV or video recorded interviews). The wrong expression could make you look like you are guilty of something they are talking about. It could also look like you are weak and are being *beaten* by them.

Use a smile strategically to show that you are not allowing yourself to be bullied. This would be during your own answers. Be careful not to smile while the interviewer says something negative.

Getting Into an Argument

Keep calm. Don't lose your cool. Arguing and yelling was once a staple of American daytime talk shows. Unless this is the image you want to put out there, Keep Calm and Interview On.

Use this phrase: "I understand that you disagree with what I have to say, I just ask that you allow me to make my points." Responding in this manner allows you to be in complete control, and come out a winner!

Hypotheticals

If you watch politicians on chat shows or during press conferences, you will often hear the phrase "I will not speak to hypotheticals." This is a great tactic that politicians understand. Entertaining a hypothetical situation can get you into trouble.

Example:

Q: *"What would have to happen to convince the President to impose a travel ban?"*

A: *"That is a hypothetical question. I don't like to engage hypothetical questions. But I can tell you that the president is very focused on safety and he will make the right decision should this become necessary."*

Notice that this person put down the ground rules in the first half of their answer, and then gave just enough information to "tie a bow" on his or her response. You can do the same. Don't be afraid to steer away from hypotheticals.

The Bait and Switch

In this scenario you think the interview is about one topic but it turns out to be about another (topic). Sometimes this is premeditated. Sometimes it isn't.

At one time, during my career as a television producer, I booked and produced celebrity segments. After booking a celebrity on the show, their publicist would sometimes request that we don't ask about something sensitive (like a recent divorce or a failed movie). Some of the on-air talent were fine with the requests and others felt it damaged their journalistic integrity. I always wanted to be upfront with the handlers because I planned on working with them again. On occasion, the host agreed to steer clear of a topic, but would forget and then bring it up—pretty uncomfortable for all parties involved.

While I was not a member of the *Late Show with David Letterman* staff, I remember tuning in to an interview he had with Nicole Kidman. She had just gone through a breakup with Tom Cruise. I know, from my experiences booking celebrities, that this is not something *any* of them would like to spend their time talking about. They would like to promote their movies or TV shows and leave. This breakup had been in tabloids and on entertainment shows.

Letterman's producers might have agreed to steer clear of this topic, but as soon as he had her in the interview chair ... he started asking questions about the situation. Kidman looked shocked and a bit angry. She did her best to give charming answers, but it was obvious that this was not what she was expecting.

The *bait and switch* can be uncomfortable. Many have gotten up and walked out on the interview. That move is difficult to pull off without bringing on more unwanted attention after the interview. For most of you, you need to give a short answer attempting to *"tie a bow"* on the question and take the interviewer down another path.

Example:

Q: *"We are going to talk about your business and a big event you have coming up, but first I'd like to ask about the bankruptcy you experienced a couple of years ago."*

A: *"That was a tough situation. While customers were loving what we do and stand for, our business needed some internal restructuring. We've fixed those problems and have gone back to focusing on what we do best...Being the #1 weight loss center in Orange County."*

The Surprise at the End

I have known some interviewers to use this technique. They convince the interviewee that this is a light, safe, supportive interview. The questions for the first three quarters of the interview fall into that category. Then, at the end, the interviewer says something to the effect of "Of course, I have to ask... as you know this is something that is out there" . . . and then asks the toughest questions. The answers to these tough questions may be the only parts that make the actual interview. Make sure you are ready for the tough questions and have followed the Answer System anytime you go into an interview situation.

The Ambush

It is entirely possible that a reporter shows up and surprises you when you least expect it. You might have seen videos of reporters harassing executives walking to their car barraging them with lists of questions. All the while, the executive is trying to get to their car and avoid giving any answers. This is usually done to create *theater* and embarrass the person being interviewed. This tends to happen to people who have not responded to a crisis or are found cheating the public.

There are other types of ambush situations, too:

➤ A reporter might come up to you at a conference and just start asking questions.

➤ Someone who does not look like a reporter might walk up to you with a cell phone video camera and also start asking questions. Your reaction is very important as this can be shared with the world with one click.

➤ A reporter looking for a quote or statement rings your phone. You answer it not knowing who they are and are now part of an interview.

➤ Someone might ask a question at a town meeting. This meeting might be recorded by the organizers, or, again, by someone using their phone.

Ways to deal with the ambush interview. Saying, "No comment," or trying to get away from an interviewer only makes you look bad. If you absolutely must not give a statement, give an answer that gives them *something* that does not make you or who you may be representing look bad.

Example:

"We are not giving interviews on this issue as of now, but what I will say is that we are focused on a solution as well as the customers affected. That's all I can add to your story at this time."

This person put something out that is positive and not specific.

> It is important for me to mention that, when dealing with big crisis situations, you must go beyond the quick hints and tips in this chapter. When I work with large companies who go through training in advance of crisis situations, they have unique, customized, plans that they can use in a time of need.

If someone walks up to you asking questions or calls you on the phone when you did not expect, it is within your right to respectfully ask that they schedule an interview. One problem reporters often say is that people use this tactic and then hide or avoid the reporter. . . never giving the actual interview. This now makes you look like a liar. If you say you will schedule an interview or offer a statement, follow through on it. If you do not want to give an interview or make a statement, you can say "I am not giving interviews on this right now." Know that you run the risk of the media owning the narrative on your story.

If a reporter calls you on the phone and needs help/quotes for a story, you can ask for 10 minutes, even a half hour, however long you need to respond. Understand that they are usually on deadline and would prefer to know whether you do intend to help them with their story or request for an interview. If you are not authorized to speak to them, let them know that and point them toward an appropriate path in getting their questions answered.

If you are at a conference or other public event, taking positive questions may be completely fine. The trouble occurs when someone is asking negative questions that you do not have good answers for. Again, instead of saying no comment, give a short answer that does not make you look bad and follow it with something that explains why you will not entertain anymore questions. Thank them for their time and interest and do your best to conclude the interview . . . politely.

For example, you could say something like, *"That is not something we are talking about at this event. I appreciate your interest, but I must get back to the event."*

Town hall meetings are a bit different. This is a very appropriate time for anyone from the public to ask questions. Some citizens might be upset or act overly passionate while asking their questions. Do your best to acknowledge them, and (as authentically as you can) move to messages you would prefer to deliver. Town hall events can get a bit dicey—especially if you have upset people in the audience and/or at the microphone. Sometimes these are recorded, even on people's phones, and could end up on YouTube or social media. Just make sure to keep your cool and to encourage a calm discourse.

Silence

The silence tactic works this way: the reporter asks you a question. You give an answer. They sit silently and act as if you have more to say. Human nature is to fill the silence. Interviewees will often continue talking and start giving answers they wish they had not said.

If you are put in this position, just sit there through the silence and wait for the next question. This will ensure that you don't fall into this trap. Just know, it may feel uncomfortable to sit quietly, staring at someone, but it is strategically the best thing you can do to NOT say something you might regret.

Killed With Kindness

Some journalists can say the meanest things while sounding polite and non-combative. Often these questions begin with, "Some people are saying . . . " then follow with something negative. The journalist gets to come off as your friend, and a good journalist simply representing the opinions of others—that happen to your adversaries. Just understand that the journalist is not your friend. They are purely out to get the best story they can.

Not *Exactly* Traps

You get a basic question, but you get upset anyway. This is not a media trap, this is you trapping yourself.

Every so often we see this happen in the news. Many times it is a celebrity or politician who does not want to talk about something already in the public discourse. Often it is a topic that is personal. Interviewers feel they must ask a "most basic question" related to the issue. Before going in front of a journalist, take a minute or two to figure out what you think the most basic questions are.

A famous example is the interview where Katie Couric asked Vice Presidential hopeful, Sarah Palin, what newspapers she read. Palin had trouble getting specific. After criticism, Palin referred to the question as a "gotcha" question. Again, this was not a trap but a situation where the interviewee had difficulty answering a particular question.

I consider a **"gotcha question"** to be something like "You say that your products are *made in America,* but, according to research we just uncovered, you are importing goods from a particular factory in the Philippines. What do you have to say to that?!"

Practice and preparation, along with telling the truth and ethical behavior, are your prescriptions for success.

WHAT IF THEY BRING UP INFORMATION YOU WERE HOPING THEY WOULDN'T?

Again, just because you were hoping they would not bring up a topic doesn't mean that they won't. Be prepared, in any media interview, to get **basic questions** concerning the story. This includes the *who, what, when, where, why, and how.* Practice using the Message and Answer System techniques, outlined earlier, and I guarantee you will feel more confident and prepared.

Video Link:

The Secret About Most Traps
Find out why most people get 'trapped" and how to avoid these situations.

www.MediaSecretsBook.com/traps

MISTAKES

"You can speak well if you tongue can deliver the message of your heart."
—JOHN FORD, DIRECTOR

No Comment

Saying, "No comment," is usually a bad idea. If you are someone within an organization that really should not be commenting, then say, "I am not the organization spokesperson. Let me put you in touch with the right person to help you out."

If you do say "No Comment," It gives the journalist nothing more than you looking guilty or like someone who is dodging questions. For those who are spokespeople, simply think of a morsel of information you can give them that doesn't necessarily answer the question, but shows, however, that you respect the process of news gathering.

Example:

"We are not giving a statement right now, but plan to once we have gone over all of the facts of this situation."

That answer will look far better to the public, and gives some small amount of satisfaction to the journalist. The journalist might still ask some follow-up questions, hoping that you will break and start commenting when you don't want to. You could always follow with, "That's all I have for now. Thank you."

Spin

Politicians and pundits are often accused of spin. *Spin* is when the interviewee tries to manipulate the facts or the direction of the story for their own gain. A politician wants you to see things their way, even if their opinions are not based on facts.

The problem is, most interviewers, and many times the audience, can you see right through this. Before social media, politicians and their handlers could get away with more of this in traditional media interviews. Now, the reaction and dissection begins instantly and continues online. It can spill back into traditional media.

Your time would be best spent creating answers using the Message System (Chapter 3) and then practicing moving to those answers with the Answer System (Chapter 4).

Off the Record

There is no such thing as off the record. If there is something that you should not be saying—don't say it! Many people have gotten burnt or been embarrassed because they said something that they thought was private and *off the record*. They might have been talking to the journalist after the interview was over. There's no reason to believe that this should be off the record. They are journalists and have the right to report anything and everything they hear and see!

Even if a journalist claimed some portion or all of your conversation to be off the record, you should still be wary of your remarks making it into the story. After all, journalists are both truth-seekers and professionals who want to deliver the "best" story they can (and that means different things for different types of reporters).

For example, some people have done TV interviews and were caught saying something they did not expect the public to hear during a commercial break, or while they were waiting for the interview to begin. Just be aware that as soon as a microphone is on you, they are often already "hot" or "open." You never know who is listening—often, it is producers in the control room. They may be all-too-willing to share what you said with the public, other writers, social media, etc. Today nothing seems private, and this is especially the case for all circumstances surrounding an interview—everything counts and you are always "on."

Defensiveness

Some people choose to allow the interviewer to rile them up. Becoming angry, acting defensive, or losing your cool, does not make you look good. Do your best to understand that the journalist's job is to ask tough questions and to create interesting content for their audience. Even if what they say is

I'm not a fan of *Spin*. I don't teach it. It is based on manipulation or deception and that is not the brand of media training I teach. This is much different than refocusing and steering an interview in the direction you want.

Understand common mistakes, so you don't make them.

not true, your job, in the "hot seat" (if that's how you're feeling), is to calmly and professionally speak their questions ... even if you are *feeling* like you are being interrogated. Stay calm, cool, and in control!

Not Having a Plan

Many people mistake an interview as a conversation between people. They cross their fingers and hope that everything goes well. This is not effective. It can go in either direction. As mentioned earlier in the book . . .

WINGING IT IS NOT A STRATEGY.

An interview is more than a conversation. It is a conversation where the interviewer asks questions and you are **strategically guiding them** to the answers you wish to have "show up" (in print, video, etc.) in the interview. When done correctly, the answers sound and feel authentic. The interviewer is happy, the audience is happy, and YOU are happy.

Proper planning includes deciding on media messages prior to an interview, creating a few "killer" sound bites, and being ready with Answer System techniques so you are set up for the best chance for success. This— combined with some short practice (ideally videotaped) is the secret for a positive outcome.

While you may get through an interview without any major issues, having no plan will probably cause some of these common interview blunders:

> Saying Um and Ah, like or "you know", as you figure out what it is that you want to say.
> Spending too long a time talking about some topics, and then have no time left to speak about other important points or messages.
> Talking about topics that are off-message and did not need to be in the interview.
> You appear to be stumbling around for answers and seem unprepared.
> You appear to be unconfident, nervous, or afraid.

Take five or ten minutes and make sure you have done some preparation before every interview. You will not regret the extra effort.

Facial Mistakes

You may say one thing, but your face might be saying something completely different.

Some people who have lied during media interviews have said "no" while their head shook "yes." Some people have pained expressions on their face. Others open the interview by saying "thanks for having me. I am happy to be here" while their face says the opposite. Most often, this is not because they are lying—they are just nervous.

Practicing with a video recording device will help you to see what the rest of the world sees.

Take time to see if your face is sending the right or wrong message.

Video Link:

Common Mistakes

What are some of the most common mistakes? Hear about them in this short video.

www.MediaSecretsBook.com/mistakes

MEDIA AS MARKETING
Secrets for Creating Momentum

"You wouldn't worry so much about what others think of you if you realized how seldom they do."
—ELEANOR ROOSEVELT

Media can be powerful marketing.

Why Most Media Trainers Don't Cover This

Unfortunately this is still off the radar for many. Traditionally, media training as a profession has focused on working with "reporters," body language, messaging, and crisis management as its top goals. However, these days the average client has their own unique set of goals. It often includes brand building, driving people to their website, and selling something—whether it be a book, a product, an idea, etc. Today, we have more access than we have ever had to the masses with outlets like YouTube, Facebook Live, social media, news sites, and other Internet options. So, if you are not taking **full** advantage of the myriad of media outlets (literally available at your fingertips), you are missing out on a huge opportunity to harness the power of these amazing opportunities.

Many get frustrated because they have trouble getting media interviews *(see Chapter 2)* or have gotten interviews but they haven't sold any product/driven web traffic. In other words, they failed to *convert* their **interviews** into definable actions like sales, email sign-ups, etc.

CONVERSION IS WHERE THE ROI IS.

Let's look at your *ROI*, your **Return On Investment**. To get a return, you must put specific effort toward that goal. While some of you may have retained a publicist and are paying them to create the media opportunities, the *conversion* is the job of the person being interviewed… you!

Steps to a Successful ROI

Step 1) Approach every interview knowing that this could be a powerful marketing piece on your website, in your printed marketing materials, or across the Internet.

Step 2) Think in advance about what an ideal interview would look like on your site.

Step 3) Practice saying what you *wish* would be in the final product, and do so on video, so you can see firsthand what is working and what needs improvement.

Step 4) Give the producers, or whoever booked the interview, materials like a suggested Q & A, a bulleted fact list, and what it is that you are hoping to promote or "plug." *(See Chapter 6 for my new definition of a media* **P.L.U.G.***.)*

You can include this sentence just before giving your ***P.L.U.G.***:

If you would be gracious enough to give a brief plug, it would be appreciated. This is what you could use:

Then include something short and not overly promotional.

Example:

"Jess Todtfeld's new book, *Media Secrets,* is out and he is giving away "7 Key Secrets When Working With the Media" to our viewers today. You can find them at MediaSecretsBook.com.

Read the ***P.L.U.G.*** out loud to someone else. Often, what we think is ready needs to be simplified and trimmed down.

Step 5) If possible, have an informal chat with the interviewer prior to the actual interview. This is where you can establish rapport. You can also ask, "Do you think it would be alright to mention my book and say that it is at the website of the same name?" The beauty of this is that they'd have to reject you to your face, so 99% of the time they will say, "Sure." Your chances of getting more time giving the ***P.L.U.G.*** increase when you give away a value item.

Step 6) During the interview make sure you are giving plenty of value and takeaway. This makes the media outlet happy because they know their audience is engaged and being given great content. They will usually reward you by giving you a ***P.L.U.G.***.

Step 7) Have a *Call to Action.* This is very important. If you leave this part out, the audience will likely not ACT. You must tell people what to do and where to go.

Example:

"I'm here at CBS in Houston and excited to talk about my dieting secrets. I'm going to give 3 big ones away right now. **Go get your** *free Top 10 download from "LoseWeightSecrets.com." But first, there are some specific next steps …*

More on Conversion

Conversion is about moving the audience from the interview to the next step, whatever you hope that next step might be. **You want to "convert" eyes or ears to clicks . . . or dollars spent.**

The best way to do this is to give something irresistible. This is where the free item comes in. You will want mention, in a non-pushy way, that you have something the audience might find valuable.

Example:

Jess: *"I have a list of the 10 most common job interview mistakes, Kathy. People can get it free from my website.*

Interviewer: *"What is that site so people can get it?"*

Jess: *"It's at www.PRsecretWeapons.com.*

Interviewer: *"Great!"*

When the audience goes to that page, in order to get this high-value, free item, **they should be required to give their first name and email.** Many online marketers call this an *ethical bribe.* You are giving them something valuable in exchange for their email address.

When you capture email addresses, you can continue to reach out/market to them. By the way, this does not mean spam them with advertisements. Here is what you should do instead:

Set up a stream of at least eight other emails, spread out, that contains additional valuable information. You can promote your product along the side or bottom, but to do this properly, you should be **leading with value**. You will build that all-important, *like, know,* and *trust*. Once you have done that, you have a much better chance of converting them into clients or customers.

You can also **invite them** to subscribe to a monthly, bimonthly, weekly, or even daily email. My philosophy is to ***not*** name it a *Newsletter*. Everyone has one of those. Name it something, interesting and unique— something they will find irresistible and want to read.

Invite them to follow you on your social networks. The key word to everything I'm mentioning here is ***Invite***. Adding people to other email lists or social networks without permission is an easy way to erode *like, know and trust*.

Combine value with offers. Many *social selling experts* suggest having a full solicitation every 4th or 5th email. The main thing to keep in mind is to be seen as someone who is always sharing valuable information. People are left wondering "If that's what I get for free, I can only imagine what the paid content/service/product must be like."

Convert them. Again, we are moving people from interviews into becoming a customer, buyer or client. Another great technique is to get people to buy something . . . even at a low price. Many offer a product or download for $1 or $7 so people can get used to buying something from you. When they've done it once, it is less of a stretch to do it again.

Move them to a higher priced product. After people buy once from you, they are more likely to buy again. If they felt value was there the first time, they are more likely to feel fine about spending more on what you have to offer.

The Up-sell. Many know this as the "You want fries with that" approach. This is where you offer something after making a sale. For those who sell information products, you might *up-sell* people to a package that includes an audio learning product or DVD set. Sometimes it is called the *One Time Offer*. There are some great programs/products that can help you with this. They include: ClickFunnels, Infusionsoft, and LeadPages.

Your Website Landing Pages and Sales Funnels. Landing pages are some other *tools of the trade.* They are like mini websites for selling a product or service or simply exchanging value for email addresses. The programs and products mentioned above can help you build them in less time and with less effort. You can also find a designer on odesk.com, upwork.com, or fiverr.com who can help you get these pages finished and working. **A *Landing Page* or *Squeeze Page* is a page that people land on.** They give their name and email in exchange for something valuable enough … to give their name and email.

Next they move to a sales page. This has information about what you are ultimately selling. Ideally it includes testimonials and benefits as well as the features. After that there is an Order page and then a Thank You or confirmation page. Just like a funnel, you start with many (people in this case) at the top and as they work their way through the pages, a smaller percentage is left at the bottom.

> Need a solution for creating landing pages or sales funnels so you convert interviews?
> Visit **www.MediaSecretsBook.com/funnels**

Your website or sales funnel is a key ingredient in the *converting interviews* process. Moving people from interviews to your website gets them checking you out and what you do. Again, a key piece is collecting emails so you can keep the conversation going.

Your website can also contain videos, audios, and links to everything else you do.

Value

You may notice that I keep stressing this. Being someone who is known for always delivering value is something that will help you build credibility and a relationship with your audience.

Here are just a few things you can do to build and share value:

➢ Add downloadable Top 10 lists
➢ Add articles

➤ Add a blog
➤ Interview others and post as either text, audio or video
➤ Create infographics
➤ Give eBooks or free lists that can help your audience

What Do You Know About Sales?

Let's face it, we are all selling something. If it is not a product, then it is an idea or some extension of ourselves (our services, our time, etc.). If you have never studied *sales,* it is time to buy a book or take a course. What you will learn will be invaluable and will trickle over to every other area of your life. Selling is about understanding people. **The best kind of selling is when you are fulfilling a need or solving a problem.** This is a sweet spot which allows you to help more people. This takes away any pressure you might feel over the selling process.

Recommended books on Sales

The Psychology of Selling by Brian Tracy
The Little Red Book of Selling by Jeffrey Gitomer
What's Your $ales$ DNA? by John Palumbo
Selling 101 by Zig Ziglar
and the classic that is a must read …
Think and Grow Rich by Napoleon Hill

Put the Completed Interviews on Your Website

I have to admit, I have often been slow with this (but reap the benefits when I follow my own advice).

Take your completed interviews, TV, Radio, Print or Internet media interviews, and post them on your website. Always make sure to download a copy as a backup. Many media outlets take content off their site after a certain amount of time. I learned that one the hard way too.

This part of the process is actually **a very important piece of the puzzle.** More of your potential or current clients will see your interviews on your website or through your own marketing channels than when it originally ran. I was interviewed on *The Daily Show* in 2009. My prospects and clients still stumble across it on my site and ask me about it.

Shoot a Behind-the-Scenes Video

Shoot a video in the greenroom. This is a great way to get an extra bonus from a media interview. You can use your smartphone and just talk about how great it is to be at this media outlet. You can mention what you'll be talking about and do all the plugging you want. You might even run into the host and end up interviewing them. (Just don't ambush them.) Some media outlets love the extra exposure. Some have rules against outsiders recording on their premises— so follow their rules.

This video can live on your website, YouTube, and be fed out on Facebook Live or other social media channels.

Think about other *behind the scenes* videos you could shoot. It could be of you preparing for an interview and talking in-depth about what you plan to say. This can be posted to YouTube and social media. It often gets more attention than the actual interview. And . . . it contains everything you were hoping to say.

Let Your Social Network Know That You Just Did an Interview

Don't forget to post updates about your media interviews on social media. When you do this—post updates about your media interviews—people start to see you as someone who the media finds credible. They see that your content is so worthy that it attracts—in a good way—attention/interviews from the media. The more they see your activity, the more they feel you are the real deal and possibly worth working with. You will also find that others with podcasts or other platforms invite you as a guest. This has happened to me and often I've sold more through those *nontraditional* channels.

Harness the Power of Social Proof

Social proof is a conclusion we draw based on the behavior of others. If you were buying a book from amazon.com, you'd check reviews to see what the "social" crowd was saying. If a friend gives you a recommendation on a movie, you value what they and others say as proof that something is what it says it is.

Interviews are a form of social proof. Just being interviewed by any outlet, big or small, is an implied endorsement by that outlet. Putting the actual interview on your website and social media outlets is social proof that you are worthy of interviews. Putting the logos on your website, under a label that says "As seen on" or "As featured on," fans the flames of social proof.

HANDLING SPECIFIC TYPES OF INTERVIEWS & MEDIA OUTLETS

"We must never settle for "good enough," because good is the enemy of great."
—TONY HSIEH, ZAPPOS CEO

TV (Live Interview)

First, find out how long your interview will be. Many live morning shows or "chat" show interviews tend to be three or six minutes long. Cable news or panel discussion interviews could last the same or the entire show. This is important information as it allows you to strategize on how to best use your time. If you have a longer amount of time, you can share more stories or examples. If you have a short amount of time, you will want to make sure you get your most important messages into answers right away. Once you know how long your interview is, you can practice seeing how many of your answers could fit in the allotted time.

Don't count on the station having makeup for you. Be prepared with your own makeup.

Will there be a pre-interview discussion? If so, the producer will write up notes for the host to follow based on your conversation. Without it, the interviewer might take the conversation in any direction. Rely on the skills and strategies that you have learned in this book to guide you during the pre-interview.

No pre-interview? Give them a *suggested Q & A* sheet. If they see interesting answers, they will likely use your questions.

Where should you look? Look at the interviewer unless instructed otherwise. If you are interviewed via satellite or via videoconference, you should look directly into the camera.

Don't be scared when you hear the term *live*. It is cost-effective for many news shows and chat shows to record or air the program as it is happening. Even taped shows are done "as live" to avoid editing and save money. Just focus on giving great content and plenty of value to their audience.

TELEVISION

News Package / Local News

News programs (and this includes the comedy/variety news shows) often put together *packages* which are self-contained, recorded news reports. There is a "formula" to putting a news package together. First, the reporter decides what they think the story is. Then they go about telling that story. For example, if they were covering a local fire, they would give the viewer the facts surrounding the fire. They would include pictures/video of the fire over the voice track. They might then tell the story through a voice-over, (Voice *over* the images) or on-camera report at the location. The last component might be quotes or sound bites from individuals, witnesses, and/or officials who can add more information or emotion to the story.

If the reporter is interviewing you for a package, many of your answers will be synthesized into their voice-over script. You may only get one or two of your answers, or on-camera quotes, into the story. Use the Sound Bite Quote System to maximize your chances of getting your quotes into the story.

Press Conferences

At some point, you may be called upon to speak to multiple members of the press at one time. This is considered a *press conference.* You may do this standing in front of a lectern, filled with microphones. You may do this on a conference call, with many reporters on the line. But no matter how this is done, you need to go into it with a plan or strategy.

There are usually two parts to this kind of interview/media event.

Part one: You will be delivering facts and information. Write out what answers you plan to deliver to the media. You get to read them. Practice reading them out loud.

Part two: You will be answering questions. To do a great job during press conferences you should:

> ➤ Be ready to use the Answer System while dealing with Q & A.
> ➤ Practice, ideally while being video recorded, to see what works and what needs to be improved. Better to make a mistake or say the wrong thing during practice than in front of people.

Here's more to help you with this type of media situation:

Opening statement. Make sure you have an opening statement that covers all of the important points and messages you really want to be in the story. Make sure not to speak too quickly. You want reporters writing down answers that you have chosen to include. You can also include elements from the Sound Bite System. Ideally, they get their top quotes from this section of your press conference.

Set ground rules. Make sure reporters know how long the press conference will last. When it is time for questions let them know how long you are available—you might be allowing ten minutes of questions, or just two minutes. If the question and answer period needs to come to a conclusion, let them know that you are only taking one or two more questions and then must head to another appointment. It is important to let the media know what to expect.

Exit strategy. Even though you let people know you are on the last question and that you plan to leave after answering it, some will usually keep asking questions until you end the press conference. If you are starting to get very uncomfortable, you can let people know that you are about to take a last question. After giving your answer, say "thank you" and leave. You are in control of ending this event.

Multiple interviewers. In most interviews, you have only one interviewer. In a press conference you are fielding questions from many different people. (This can also be the case in some TV and radio interviews, as well.)

A big difference with multiple interviewers is that questions are divided up among different people. Try not to stress over this aspect. You are still being asked one question at a time. Use all the same techniques you have learned and practiced.

Satellite TV interview / Remote Style Interview

An interview *via satellite* or via remote usually means that the interviewer is in one camera location and the interviewee is asked to be at a second camera location. This could be opposite sides of the world or opposite sides of the same studio. (Skype interviews and the web-based version of this situation are also covered in this chapter.)

The main thing you need to know is that you will be required to look at the camera instead of the person interviewing you. You might be looking into the lens. It is entirely possible that the lens is hidden behind teleprompter glass. In that case, you might be looking at a big dark square or video of the program as it is happening.

What I advise clients to do, when they are faced with this type of interview situation, is to pretend they are talking to someone who is very excited about everything they have to say. This way, you feel like everything you say is being well-received by an actual human. Some stations will attach a little drawing of a happy face and tell people to just look at the drawing (which is just below the camera's lens). This works too, but you

must make sure that you are giving back charismatic facial expressions and body language.

RADIO

The great thing about radio interviews is that you can keep some notes in front of you. Never read directly from your notes. Unfortunately, most people *sound* like they are reading. Use bullet points and large fonts so you can glance and easily take in the information.

In-Studio Interviews

While many radio interviews are done over the phone, often guests are asked to come into the studio for an interview. The radio station likes this the most because they have control over the quality of audio.

Try to find out, in advance, how long the show is and how long your interview is. These are two different lengths. Even if you are told that you are the guest for a half-hour section of the program, the interview might be broken up with commercials, news, sports, traffic reports or other content. Do your best to be as helpful as you can with the interview and to deliver the best, most value driven, content that will be helpful to the audience.

Call-In Interviews

As mentioned in Chapter 8, calling in on a landline is preferred. Having a crisp connection and a call that will not drop out is as important (if not more important) than your content. If your audio is subpar, your interview will be cut short.

Always remember, your job, with any type of radio interview, is to deliver great information that their audience will love. Many people will say that they love this type of interview because they can deliver the interview in their home, even from their bed. Unfortunately, if you do that, you might sound like you are actually sleepy and/or lying down. I recommend having tea or water prior to the interview. Standing up will also help you sound your best during the interview.

See my top 10 list for doing radio interviews (Chapter 14).

Drive Time

Many people listen to the radio while commuting to and from work. The shows that broadcast during this time are called "drive time" shows. They tend to mix news with comedy and audience interaction. They can be wacky and irreverent. Always do your research (prior to any interview) to find out what the show is known for—i.e., topics typically covered, the host's style, personality, and how respectful they are to their guests. Most are, but some will "goof" on their interviewees (so it's important to be prepared).

Drive time shows are desirable because they tend to have a larger audience share. Just make sure to do your homework first, and do right by their audience.

The Package Interview

Just like in television, radio has its own version of a "package" interview. This is where they combine a reporter's script or narration with quotes and sound bites from people they interview. It is important for you to use the Sound Bite Quote System when delivering this type of interview. While they still want facts from you, the pieces of your interview that will make it into the final cut are your actual quotes.

Internet Radio

This type of interview includes podcasts, blogtalkradio.com interviews, interviews recorded over a conference call… all usually shared through an Internet platform.

All of the rules apply from other types of interviews, especially radio. Note that there are some big benefits to doing this kind of interview. These interviews tend to be highly segmented. That means that they appeal to a very specialized audience. If this is an audience you are trying to reach, it is a fantastic place for you to show up.

These interviews are often very shareable. Make sure to share with your social media friends and followers. This will get you noticed by the host/producers of the show. It will also make you more attractive as someone they will want to ask back on the show.

PRINT

Being seen in a newspaper article still holds high credibility with those who read it. Often, these interviews are done over the phone. Make sure you have prepared with your Message System grid, and that your sound bites/quotes are written out and ready to go. Reporters will usually talk to you longer when they are hunting around for a good quote. If you give them some great quotes early on in the interview, they will appreciate it and get what they need in a shorter amount of time. You will also appreciate it if they use your **exact quote** (or quotes) that you took the time to write down in advance of the interview.

If you've alerted the press to a story (or sent them a pitch) and you think you might get phone calls on the go, asking for quotes and commentary, you can keep a sheet with your sound bites in your pocket so you feel prepared anywhere.

Newspapers: National and Local

These days, everything is national and international. Most articles appear in the written newspaper for a day. But, they live on, through the newspaper's website, for anywhere from a month to years. Local interviews can often be easier to get and can lead to national interviews or other opportunities.

Misquotes

Many people worry that they will be taken out of context or misquoted. Just be careful not to repeat any premises you don't agree with. Make sure you clarify anything you think the reporter did not understand. Sticking to your messages and using your quotes that you've written out will give you the most control, and the best shot at seeing the answer you desire in the article.

Magazines

These outlets usually need three or more months lead time when creating articles. All of the rules apply when speaking to this type of print reporter. The stories tend to be longer in length. This just means that your interview might be longer. Since they have more time to work on the story, you may get asked numerous times for more information or facts. Just make sure you are easy to work with and a help to the reporter. This is the type of thing they remember and think of when they are looking for help with future stories.

Ezines, Blogs, E-Newsletters, and Electronic Media

Don't discount what you think are smaller media outlets. Remember, these types of outlets appeal to very specific groups and demographics. If you are somebody who wants to be heard by financial advisors, being interviewed by a blog, where the primary readers are financial advisors, is the right place to show up. Newsletters that go out to the membership of an organization you want to connect with are also great place for you to show up.

Sometimes these outlets will even ask you to write an article they can use. I was asked by *Speaker* Magazine, a magazine put out by the National Speakers Association, to write an article on attracting media attention. Not only did they use every word I wrote, they asked for pictures and ended up putting me on the cover. This is great because this magazine reaches meeting planners and others who might poke me to give paid speeches. The moral of the story—you can have more control than you think in this area.

INTERNET VIDEO

Skype, Zoom, FaceTime, YouTube, & Hangout Interviews

These days, anyone can decide to be an interviewer. This includes you! This can be an opportunity to learn more about anyone you admire and want to connect with.

This type of interview is done over Webcam or sometimes via smartphone. The interviews can be short or long. While you may think that these types of interviews may not have the same cachet as a traditional media outlet, again, they can easily be shared on social media and be seen by the people you want to be seen by.

These types of interviews are usually a straight question & answer format, but give way to acting and behaving outside of the box. Often they can be extremely authentic and not be bound by a media outlet's point of view or format.

Facebook Live / Periscope

Newer to the scene, as of the writing of this book, are Facebook Live, Periscope and Meerkat. YouTube is playing catch up on the *live stream* excitement. These outlets offer you a direct video connection with the public. With the download of their app on your smartphone, you can quickly broadcast an interactive (i.e. the audience can text or post questions or comments) live stream with nothing more than your phone. This medium is more about being interactive and consistent in delivering content.

The benefits of using these mediums are still being seen. David Newman, author of *Do It! Marketing* says "using new platforms to meet new people is always a good thing."

At this point, the new trend is live streaming your own content directly to an audience. Think of it the way celebrities and politicians use Twitter. To avoid looking like someone who rambles incessantly, try to show up with an agenda or list of items you hope to cover—so that you deliver top-notch content to your audience.

Kid Reporter

Webinars

While the definition of webinars tends to be a web delivered broadcast, usually PowerPoint with someone speaking over it, the definition needs to be expanded. I see webinars as any type of seminar delivered via the Internet. You can use any of the broadcast outlets and methods mentioned above or use something like GoToWebinar, WebEx, Adobe Connect, ReadyTalk, Webinar Ninja and AnyMeeting. Each has different features that include polling, use of webcam, screen-sharing, and taking calls and questions, among other features.

While I have delivered full-day programs on the best way to use this one particular platform, the most important points include:

➢ Think about the type of broadcast you might actually watch as a viewer and stick with that.
➢ Are you taking 15 minutes to introduce the whole broadcast? Make sure to deliver massive value, straight out of the gate.

➤ Are there other ways for you to be interactive? The audience enjoys being a part of the discussion. It also keeps them awake and listening. Will showing your Webcam, meaning your face, enhance the program? As an audience member, we appreciate seeing those who are speaking to us. Often, as the speaker, we prefer to hide and not show our face. Which option best supports your particular goals? Get feedback from others after you have delivered a webinar or web broadcast.

➤ Force yourself to watch a recording of your webinar. If you find yourself tuning out or looking away, imagine what your audience must be doing. Make the necessary changes so your audience has a reason to return.

Always take a few minutes to research the outlet that will be interviewing you.

YOUR QUICK START GUIDE

"Action breeds confidence and courage."
—DALE CARNEGIE

Most pieces of electronic equipment come with a quick start guide—why can't *all* areas of life come with such a handy guide to operation/best practices? .

This section is designed to give you a **quick start** for the most common types of interviews or media situations. Below, you will find top 10 lists—strategies—that will prepare you for the most common types of interviews.

Have you listened to the free quick start audio that came with this book? If not, you'll want to check it out. It is designed to help get you started and take action as quickly as possible.

Special Chapter Note: If you represent an organization that has a communication policy or compliance issues, you need to know it and stick to it. You may need to have all outside interview communications go through someone else, and get approvals before speaking to the media.

TELEVISION

TV Interviews

1. Lean forward 15 degrees toward the camera when doing a "sit-down" interview. (This gets rid of, or reduces, the "camera adds 10 pounds" effect.)

2. Look at the interviewer (not the camera), unless instructed to do otherwise during special circumstances.

3. Body Language: Move your hands, head, and body.
   This way you will look more natural, calmer, and more confident. As the interview goes on, you will start to feel that way, too.

4. Prior to the interview, write out a list of answers you would love to say in an ideal situation.

5. Divide them into three categories and transfer it onto the **message grid**. Give each category a one word heading. These are your Media Messages. This is your road map for the interview. It will make a dramatic change to your ability to get exact messages/answers into the interview.

6. To stay "on-message," stay focused on just three categories of messages. Three popular categories are: **Problem, Solution, and Call to Action.**

7. Wear solids (but not black, white, or bright red). No shiny or noisy jewelry that can distract attention.

8. Energy! Energy! Energy! Make sure you have great energy. Be passionate about your topic. It will be infectious.

9. Offer real value to the audience. If you do that, people will want to find out more about who you are and your topic.

10. PLUGGING. Don't forget about your needs! If you are trying to get more traffic to your web site, promote a product or book, or mention your business, WEAVE it into an answer. Blurting out a web site and not giving anyone a reason to go there is not a technique that will make the media like you, or drive audiences to your website. Plugging an irresistible, free item that can be downloaded from your website offers value and gives the interviewer a reason to let you mention your site . . . likely more than once.

Radio

1. Write out ten bullet points you plan to say during the interview. Email it to the producer and/or host. Chances are good that they'll use it as their guide.
2. Write out a larger list of answers you would love to say in an ideal situation.
3. Divide them into three categories and transfer it onto the message grid. This will make them easier to bring up.
4. Have your message grid (sheet) in front of you during the interview. Use some of those messages. (Don't sound like you are reading.)
5. If possible, stand up. Move around (if possible). It will add energy to your voice. (Only do this if doing the interview via phone.)
6. Use your hands when you speak. It will improve the quality of your voice.
7. Be passionate about your topic. If you're not excited about it, no one else will be.
8. When doing an interview over the phone—use a landline! (Landlines have clearer reception than cell phones and you don't have to worry about your call being dropped.)

9. Have a point of view. Radio producers and hosts like that. They may even ask you back.

10. Offer a "Takeaway." Ask yourself, what will the audience take away from the segment? Is there real value that will have them remembering you and possibly wanting more?

Bonus Tips:

11. If this is a longer interview, have some interesting stories ready that support your points/messages.

12. Sell without selling… Make sure you have a "call to action." What actions should people take?

13. If the interview is "in studio," confirm the interview the night before and show up at least a half hour early. They will likely consider you a "low-maintenance" guest.

14. Be prepared with a "killer" first answer. Often the first question will be some version of, "(Can you tell us about this your new project, book, topic?")

15. If doing the interview over the phone, disable call waiting. (Dial *70 first on US landlines.)

16. Turn off cell phones, turn down your radio (if listening in) and quiet any other surrounding noise.

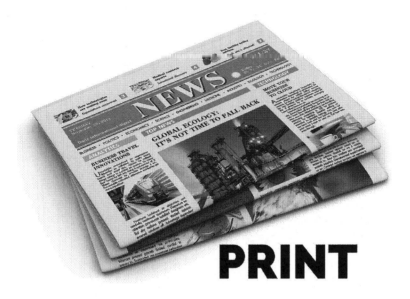

Print

1. Know that print reporters absolutely, positively, want one thing from you . . . QUOTES. Come up with some short, tight, answers.
2. Before the interview, write out the answers (or messages) you would like to have in the interviews.
3. Divide those answers you just wrote into three categories and transfer them onto the Media Messaging Grid. This will make them easier to bring up.
4. For phone interviews: keep the **Media Messaging Grid** in front of you. If you are face-to-face with the reporter, then think of the three titles at the top of the grid. Those three words are your *mental roadmap* toward bringing up messages.
5. Practice at least once, aloud, with another person interviewing you. Record/review it. If you don't do this, you won't feel like you are warmed-up until the real interview has concluded. If you do practice once before, you will already be warmed-up, and feel prepared, come interview time.

6. Use your body language, especially your hands, even over the phone. This will help make you feel more relaxed, and improve the quality of your voice. And, in person, you'll look more natural (using your hands/body language during the interview).

7. Energy! Energy! Energy! Make sure you have great energy. Be passionate about your topic. It will be infectious.

8. Know that anything that comes out of your mouth could be used as a quote. Don't repeat phrases from the reporter that you don't want to see as your quote.

9. If you hear the reporter typing or get very quiet, slow down and let them write out your quotes. Their silence can be a good thing.

10. Know that everything you say is "on the record." This includes any pre-chatting or interview post-chatting.

Last thoughts. If a reporter calls: First, work out the protocol for keeping your publicist or communication person in the loop. They might have strategies, advice, or warnings you need to hear. As for the reporter, they are usually on deadline. If you are not available to speak, they will likely move on to the next person who can help them. If you want to take time to create some perfect answers, you can tell them that you are absolutely available but want to finish up what you are working on. Ask if you can do the interview in ten minutes. This will give you time to write out your main messages and answers you'd like to deliver during the interview.

Do you want to have some control over exactly how they describe you and what you do? Give them **your one sentence description.** Often they print it word for word. For example, *Jess Todtfeld, President of Success In Media, is a NY-based media consultant.*

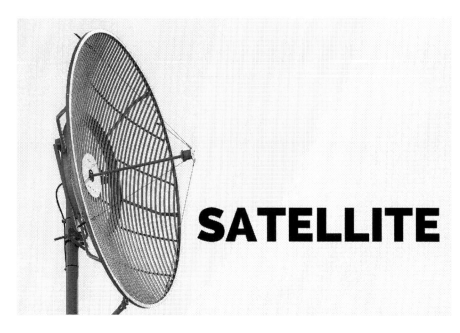

Satellite Media Tour

1. Before the interview, write out the answers (or messages) you would love to deliver in the interviews.
2. Divide them into three categories and transfer it onto the message grid. This will make them easier to bring up.
3. Practice looking into a video camera and pretending like you are having a conversation with a real person. (Video recording with your cell phone or web cam works well as video camera. If you have never done a satellite TV interview, practice is imperative.)
4. Sit on the edge of your seat and lean forward 15%. This will decrease the "camera adds 10 pounds" effect.
5. Use your body language, especially your hands. This will make you appear more natural. Practice using your hands in the top half of your chest. This way it will be in the camera's view.
6. Energy! Energy! Energy! Make sure you have great energy. If you are not passionate about your topic, viewers won't be either.
7. Know that anything you do while in the interview chair could be broadcast. This means you might be on when the interviewer is busy talking to someone else, or when questions are being asked.

8. Give a slight "TV Smile" during questions. It looks like you are a pleasant person and are happy to be there. Use that smile during your introduction—so you don't have the "deer in the headlights" look.

9. If the ear piece, a.k.a. IFB (Interruptible Feedback Device), pops out of your ear, calmly adjust it and push it back in. The best time to do this is when it is your turn to talk.

10. When the host says, "Thanks for being here," in the beginning or end of the segment, say "Thanks" or "Thank you." Some people just sit their silently and it gets awkward.

Bonus Tip:

11. After you think the interview has ended, know that you might still be on camera. Don't roll your eyes, jump out of your seat, use profanity or anything you wouldn't intentionally want on camera. Wait until you are **1000%** sure that you are not being broadcast, and then STILL make sure you calmly remove your mic, ear piece, and walk away (calmly).

Internet/Blog/Social Media

1. Know What You're Dealing With. Internet journalists often have little or no training as an interviewer. This works to your advantage. Know that they are often looking for one thing specifically: having you say something interesting! They may have an agenda. Look around their blog, prior to the interview, so that you are prepared.

2. Questions. Often, bloggers will just send you a list of ten questions. Wow. Talk about control! While you don't have to worry about being misquoted in that situation, make sure you are not too bland or self-promotional. Use this as an opportunity to excite readers and have them search for you.

3. The Google Factor. Know that the interview will live on and be "searchable" on the Internet. This is a good thing. This means traditional journalists might find you, while researching, and ask for an interview.

4. Be Quotable. Know that, like print reporters, they absolutely, positively, want one thing from you . . . QUOTES. Come up with some short, tight answers. Use the Sound Bite Quote System.

5. Tell Good Stories. They might print/run the entire story. This makes you more interesting, draws in more people, and more words or

search-friendly terms—which means more chances for Google to cross-index the interview.

6. Give Helpful Facts. Give the audience real information that will make this interview stand out, be relevant, and useful.

7. Load Up Your Answers. Think in advance about some of the answers you'd like to have in the story. Write some of them down so you can increase the chances of them being used.

8. Phone Interviews: Keep that list of messages in front of you. Don't sound like you are reading. It is just a guide.

9. FREE. Give a free item or something of value. Web journalists are fine with promoting your web address, but this will motivate their audience to actually visit your site.

10. Energy! Energy! Energy! Make sure you have great energy. Be passionate about your topic. It will be infectious.

FINAL SECRETS

Here we are at the end of the book, but at the beginning of your journey.

There has never been a better time in the world to be in control of your own messages and to be able to reach as many or the right people.

If you have something to say . . . say it.

The biggest obstacle, is . . . you. Reaching people through "mass media" is all here for the taking. Take the opportunities or make your own.

Build momentum.

Get better over time.

Make mistakes. Get up, dust yourself off and improve.

Remember and act on the biggest lessons you learned in this book. Know that breaking through is easier than you think. Know that media folks are people too and they need your help. Leading with value is a recipe for success. You can get what you want, but you must also make sure the media outlet and audience get what they want. *Traps* are usually ones we've made for ourselves. The same can be said for opportunities.

Use a mix of traditional media tactics and self-created media tactics. Write, blog, podcast, and experiment with live Internet broadcasting. Use the tools that feel right for creating a following.

Above all, DO SOMETHING.
Take action. Inaction is the enemy of success.

Don't feel like you are completely ready to take the leap?
ACT IT and BECOME IT.

RECOMMENDATIONS

These are some of the best services out there that can help you with your media marketing.

The Celebrity Branding Agency www.CelebrityBrandingAgency.com
Want to be seen on ABC, NBC, FOX & CBS? Want to publish a bestselling book? This team knows how to brand you as the celebrity in your field.

The National Publicity Summit
www.NationalPublicitySummit.com This is like speed dating with journalists. Twice yearly, top media bookers and editors convene for this event. One hundred attendees get to pitch themselves and their topics for big exposure.

Bestseller Big Business
www.BestsellerBigBusiness.com
Trevor Crane and his team will not only help you get your book done and published, they will show you how to integrate it into a bigger marketing plan. All of this can be done authentically and allow you to help more people. The bonus? You will learn how to create massive attention and how to make your book a bestseller.

PR Secret Weapons Kit
www.PRSecretWeapons.com
This kit was put together after I set the Guinness Record for publicity. It includes videos on how to pitch and what works. Audio interviews with a Good Morning America producer, Cable News producer, CBS producer, Radio host, PR Veterans, online media stars, and those who are converting interviews into sales. The kit includes a media list of more than three thousand contacts.

Media Ready in 30 Days or Less
www.MediaReadyIn30.com
This is a video-delivered version of my in-person workshops. If you are looking to take yourself to the next level, check it out.

Productivity / Time Management www.The7MinuteLife.com/
Allyson Lewis and her entire system can ignite your productivity. You can gain a way to track what you have done in a day, get a score, and know that high value activities are being accomplished.

The Confidence Coach
www.TheConfidenceCoach.Net.au/ Is confidence something you need to work on? Kathryn Orford is your go-to professional with many options for taking yourself from funk to fantastic.

> **For more recommendations visit:**
> **www.MediaSecretsBook.com/JessRecommends**

ABOUT THE AUTHOR

Jess Todtfeld helps his clients to quickly gain the confidence and skills to master media interviews, speeches and presentations. Jess' easy to understand systems, combined with focused practice and his 365-day support and accountability program, allow clients to quickly boost their media skill set and get real results.

 Jess Todtfeld, CSP, is one of the leading communication and media training authorities in the U.S. With more than fifteen years as a media trainer and consultant, Todtfeld helps CEOs, business executives, spokespersons, public relations representatives, experts, and authors to become more confident, more in control, and to create more results from their speaking engagements and media appearances.

Todtfeld has trained clients from the United Nations, IBM, JPMorgan, AARP, USA Today, The World Children's Wellness Foundation, Land Rover USA, LinkedIn, The American College of Emergency Room Physicians, Scripps TV Networks, Gallup, North Face apparel, and the ASPCA.

He brings with him thirteen years of experience as a TV producer for NBC, ABC, and FOX, having booked and produced over 6,000 segments. Producing credits include being part of the team that launched "The O'Reilly Factor" and "FOX & Friends." Jess' time in front of the camera includes features reporting, guest spots on national/international news programs, and hosting of "America's Premiere Experts" which has been broadcast on ABC, NBC, FOX and CBS affiliates in the U.S. As a media guest, Jess set a Guinness Record for being interviewed the most times in 24 hours . . . 112 interviews on different radio stations around the world.

Made in the USA
Columbia, SC
16 August 2020